Ruth C. Wylie's two volumes of *The Self-Concept*, published by the University of Nebraska Press in 1974 and 1979, evaluated the mass of psychological and sociological studies of self-concept and self-esteem. Looking at a plethora of tests, Wylie found in 1974 that very few had been adequately conceived or implemented. Many produced results that were unverifiable or specious. Since then psychometric tests of self-concept have continued to proliferate, and Wylie has continued to assess them.

Measures of Self-Concept briefly summarizes the psychometric criteria for self-concept tests and the present general state of methodological adequacy of currently used measures, including both widely used earlier tests and some promising new ones still under development. Although Wylie still finds serious shortcomings, she notes a greater attempt today to increase and evaluate the validity of self-concept indices by more sophisticated means. She presents detailed, up-to-date information about and psychometric evaluations of ten self-concept tests that appear to be the most meritorious candidates for current use and for further research and development. The first book since her 1974 volume to review specific as well as general measures of self-esteem for a range of ages from preschool to adult, *Measures of Self-Concept* will be of major interest to self-concept researchers, clinicians, and academic dissectors of the human personality.

Ruth C. Wylie, a professor emeritus of psychology at Goucher College, has published widely in her discipline.

Ruth C. Wylie

Measures of Self-Concept

University of Nebraska Press
Lincoln and London

Copyright © 1989 by the
University of Nebraska Press
All rights reserved
Manufactured in the
United States of America

The paper in this book meets
the minimum requirements of
American National Standard for
Information Sciences—Permanence
of Paper for Printed Library Materials,
ANSI Z39.48-1984.

Library of Congress Cataloging-in-Publication Data
Wylie, Ruth C.
Measures of self-concept.

Includes index.
1. Self-perception–Testing.
2. Self-perception–Testing–Evaluation.
I. Title.
BF697.5.S43W95   1989   155.2'8   88-28038
ISBN 0-8032-4751-6

To the memory of
Katherine E. Baker
and
Georgiana R. Wylie

Contents

Acknowledgments

My thanks go to Morris Rosenberg, who encouraged me to undertake this project, and to Barker Bausell, Barbara Byrne, Herbert Marsh, and Olive Quinn, who read all or parts of the manuscript and made many helpful suggestions.

Barbara Byrne, René L'Écuyer, Hazel Markus, Herbert Marsh, Morris Rosenberg, Roberta Simmons, and Susan Harter provided useful information to supplement my published sources. Barbara Simon provided expert help in the computer search of the literature.

Western Psychological Services has kindly granted permission to quote copyrighted items from the Piers-Harris Children's Self-Concept Scale, and Morris Rosenberg has kindly granted permission to quote items from the Rosenberg Self-Esteem Scale and the Rosenberg-Simmons Self-Esteem Scale.

I

INTRODUCTION

History, Purpose, and Scope
of the Present Work

Because theoretical and research publications on the self-concept had burgeoned after 1949, I decided in 1970 that it would be useful to try to do two things: summarize standards of measurement and research design relevant to studies of self-conceptions, and review the extant studies in order to evaluate their interpretability in the light of these methodological criteria (Wylie, 1974, 1979).

With respect to measurement, I found that most of the purported self-concept indices had been used only once or a few times, precluding evaluation of their adequacy and interpretation of the results of studies based on them. However, a few instruments had been used in a good many studies and had been subjected to some, but not all, of the relevant psychometric technologies such as item analysis, factor analysis, and controls for response set. Fourteen of these instruments representing different formats and aimed at different aspects of self-conceptions were selected for detailed consideration in light of all relevant criteria for psychometric adequacy. The best of them had fulfilled quite a few of the requirements for psychometric adequacy, but several were judged to be seriously deficient and hence not to be recommended (Wylie, 1974).

Since the 1974 and 1979 reviews, the flood of research directed toward phenomenological or conscious self-conceptions has continued, and self-esteem in particular has been considered by both laypersons and professionals to be of great importance in accounting for human behavior and to be a function of a very wide array of variables. Thus, questions of methodological adequacy are still important.

The general criteria for such adequacy are the same as those extensively discussed in Wylie (1974) and other sources, so these criteria, together with useful methodological references concerning them, are simply listed below. Important changes have occurred, however, with respect to the state of instrument development.

In view of these changes in extant measures, it seems worthwhile to present and evaluate both some of the previously discussed instruments that have undergone further development and some promising new instruments that are still undergoing development. My aim was to choose a variety of measures researchers might find useful, either as bases for further psychometric development or as appropriate indices of variables they wish to include in their substantive researches.

Some of the new measures are only briefly mentioned, not formally analyzed, because sufficient psychometric information is not yet available. They are alluded to below because readers may wish to pursue their psychometric development and application.

It is still true that part of the problem in establishing and evaluating the psychometric adequacy of any measure of self-conception lies in the vague state of theorizing in the self-concept domain. However, in the present work I do not repeat previous systematic discussions of theorizing, and readers may wish to refer to Wylie (1968, 1974, 1979), Kihlstrom and Cantor (1984), and Shavelson, Hubner, and Stanton (1976).

Sources of Information Concerning Extant Instruments

To update my knowledge about which of the pre-1974 instruments are still in use and what new ones are under development, I began by making a computer inquiry of Dialog as to the number of publications that appeared between 1978 and 1986 inclusive under any one of the following thesaurus terms: *body image, gender identity, self-acceptance, self-concept,* and *self-esteem.* The answer was 16,951 for the self-referent words, 1,452 for body image, and 443 for gender identity!

Since the concerns addressed here are psychometric, not substantive, I requested a cross between any of the terms above and *concurrent validity, construct validity, content validity, discriminant validity, convergent validity, face validity, test-item analysis, test-item content, test reliability, factor analysis,* and *multitrait-multimethod matrix.* Although there were 10,938 publications with one or more of these method terms, the crossing of all the listed self-referent terms with all the listed method terms yielded only 455 titles.

It seems clear that the ratio of methodological work to substantive research was at least as low as I had found it to be between 1949 and 1977.

Only about half of the 455 abstracts mentioned a specific instrument by name, for example, the Rosenberg Self-Esteem Scale or the Tennessee Self-Concept Scale. Since I had previously found that most studies up through 1977 used idiosyncratic instruments about which little or no psychometric information was available, I surmised that this unfortunate practice must still be frequent. However, limitations of time and money precluded checking this impression by going to the many articles for which the abstract mentioned no specific self-referent test. Therefore I have probably missed some information about more developed tests.

As a second way of locating and evaluating possible tests for inclusion here, I examined *Personality Tests and Reviews* (Buros, 1970) and the seventh, eighth, and ninth *Mental Measurements Yearbooks* (Buros, 1972, 1978; Mitchell, 1985), where commercially available instruments are described and evaluated. I also searched commercial test catalogs for further candidates for inclusion and examined test manuals and specimen sets of any that seemed appropriate and meritorious.

If the *Mental Measurements Yearbook* reviewers and I agreed on either a positive or a negative evaluation of a commercially available test, it was accordingly included (or excluded) from consideration here.

Finally, from my general reading of recent literature, I selected some instruments that appeared to me to be entering new territory, and I sought, with limited success, to obtain information from the authors if that were needed in order to evaluate the psychometric status of such instruments.

Criteria for Inclusion of Instruments

Besides general methodological promise, another criterion for inclusion was the author's stated intent to create a self-report index of self-concept. Although many of the widely used and extensively developed personality tests also consist of self-report items, thus being operationally similar to purported self-concept tests, their purpose is not to infer self-conceptions, but rather to classify respondents into empirical categories such as diagnostic groups (e.g., the Minnesota Multiphasic Personality Inventory) or personality dimensions (e.g., Jackson's Personality Research Form). Hence they have not been considered here.

Four additional criteria for inclusion were that the tests be intended for a variety of age groups, have different formats, address a variety of relatively specific self-concept domains, and address overall self-esteem measurement from different conceptual bases.

Elsewhere (Wylie, 1974, chapter 4) I reviewed a number of instruments I have not included here, for two reasons: (1) Some of them have serious methodological shortcomings that I discussed in detail in 1974. These are Coopersmith's Self-Esteem Inventory (see also reviews in Mitchell, 1985), Gough and Heilbrun's Adjective Check List (ACL) (see also reviews in Buros, 1972, and Mitchell, 1985), Leary's Interpersonal Check List (ICL), Long and Ziller's Self-Social Symbols Test (see also Wells & Marwell, 1976, pp. 112–114), the Tennessee Self-Concept Scale (see also Bentler's, Suinn's and Crites's reviews in Buros, 1972, and Marsh & Richards, in press a), the Twenty Sentences Test (TST) or Who Are You? (WAY) (see also Wells & Marwell, 1976, pp. 114–120), various semantic differential instruments, Q-sorts, especially Butler and Haigh's version, and Worchel's

Self-Activity Inventory (SAI). (2) So far as I can tell, many of the instruments above (as well as Bills's methodologically better Index of Adjustment and Values [IAV]) have seldom been used in the past 15 years, and further psychometric development of them has not been carried out.

Instruments Briefly Mentioned

I had hoped to include a number of instruments that have come to my attention through general reading and that seem to represent new approaches.

Liveseley and Bromley (1973), Bromley (1977), L'Écuyer (1975, 1981), and McGuire and McGuire (1987) have developed new versions of the Who Are You? technique in order to address their concerns with self-concept development. Each has proposed a different specific coding system, but insufficient information is at hand to sustain a psychometric evaluation of these systems.

Intuitively, it appears that this kind of open-ended approach might yield uniquely valuable information about self-views, since it gives respondents the best possible chance to express their self-concepts in their own ways. However, the situation is more complex than it seems, and one needs to pay close attention to the particular threats to construct validity that characterize this approach (see Wylie, 1974, pp. 240–247).

This is not to say that researchers should avoid using these coding schemes; rather, more reliability and validity information is needed, and results should be interpreted in the light of important cautions.

Another line of research is being pursued by Markus and her associates (Markus & Nurius, 1986, 1987), involving the concepts of hoped-for, feared, and expected "possible selves." This set of constructs overlaps with, but is broader than, the concept of ideal self, and its authors hope that "possible selves" will provide a conceptual link between self-concept and motivation, thus leading on to predictions about behavior.

Both an open-ended and a closed-ended version of the

questionnaire have been used thus far, and work is in progress to develop the pool of possible selves for closed-format versions for specific populations.

In the original questionnaire, the sorts of possible selves included personality descriptors (e.g., creative, selfish), physical descriptors (e.g., good-looking, blind), life-style and life events (e.g., having an attractive social life, being alcohol dependent), general abilities (e.g., being able to cook well or influence people), occupational alternatives (e.g., Supreme Court justice, taxi driver), and descriptors tied to the opinions of others (e.g., being loved or feared).

Some interesting substantive findings are reported, but since information about reliability and construct validity is not available, I have not formally reviewed Markus's instruments here.

Readers may wish to consult Markus and Nurius (1986, 1987) for a general overview. The various forms of the questionnaires, and a number of published and unpublished studies that detail the coding of open-ended probes, are available from Hazel Markus, 5456 Institute for Social Research, University of Michigan, Ann Arbor, Michigan.

Instruments Formally Reviewed

Although none of the instruments formally reviewed below has yet been subjected to all the necessary test-development procedures, they all show promise of fulfilling their intended purposes. This does not mean that any of them is ready to be used as a basis for educational, diagnostic, or interventional decisions about individuals. Rather, the instruments have promise for research use.

I have tried to gather as much information as possible about every test reviewed below in order to address the following points concerning each one. (The page numbers in parentheses refer to full discussions in Wylie [1974] of what should be considered under the respective headings. Not all the issues considered in Wylie [1974] are included in this list.)

Rationale and general description
Item/scale selection and refinement (40–49)
Samples
Descriptive statistics
Reliability (117–122)
    Internal consistencey
    Test-retest
Construct validity (38–117, 299–309)
    Factor-analytic checks on dimensionality, both exploratory (97–102) and confirmatory (for useful conceptual discussions of the latter, see Briggs & Cheek, 1986; Judd, Jessor, & Donovan, 1986; Marsh & Hocevar, 1983).
    Irrelevant response/score determiners (52–95, 119–121)
    Convergent and discriminant validity (49–52)
    Multitrait-multimethod matrices (49–50, 107–116) Campbell and Fiske's (1959) original statements are vague regarding how different two instruments must be to constitute different methods, and how to evaluate the relative sizes of monotrait-monomethod (reliability) coefficients, monotrait-heteromethod (convergent validity) coefficients, heterotrait-monomethod coefficients, and heterotrait-heteromethod coefficients in order to make inferences about the convergent and discriminant validity of the measures included in the matrix. Marsh and Hocevar (1983), Wells and Marwell (1976, pp. 183–191), and Wylie (1974, pp. 107–114) have all discussed the advantages and limitations of various formal statistical methods of analyzing these matrices to evaluate convergent and discriminant validity more precisely. In this review, however, I rely on the original Campbell and Fiske specifications.
    Convergent validity coefficients (95–96)
    Assumed validity studies that examine whether the purportedly valid self-concept measure relates to other variables in a manner predicted by theory (50–51) (see also Cronbach & Meehl, 1955).

The instruments I discuss below are presented as nearly as possible in order of their date of first publication.

Piers-Harris Children's Self-Concept Scale (PH) (1964), ages 8–
    18
Rosenberg Self-Esteem Scale (RSE) (1965), high school to adult-
    hood
Rosenberg-Simmons Self-Esteem Scale (RSSE) (1972), ages 8–
    19
Joseph Pre-School and Primary Self-Concept Screening Test
    (JPPSST) (1979)
Pictorial Scale of Perceived Competence and Social Acceptance
    for Young Children (PSCA) (1983), preschool to grade 2
Self-Description Questionnaire (SDQ) (1983), ages 7–13
Self-Description Questionnaire II (SDQ II) (1985), ages 11–18
Self-Description Questionnaire III (SDQ III) (1984), late adoles-
    cent through young adult
Body Esteem Scale (BES) (1984), undergraduates
Self-Perception Profile for Children (SPPC) (1985), grades 3–8

These instruments vary greatly with respect to the amount
of information available about their development and characteristics. The two earliest ones (PH and RSE) and two of the latest
ones (SDQ and SDQ III) have been studied most fully.

2

PIERS-HARRIS CHILDREN'S SELF-CONCEPT SCALE (PH)
(Piers & Harris, 1964; Piers, 1984)

Rationale and General Description

This instrument, intended for children aged 8–18 years, comprises 80 first-person declarative statements to be answered Yes or No. The total score purports to index overall self-esteem. There are also six factorially established cluster scales labeled Behavior, Intellectual and School Status, Physical Appearance and Attributes, Anxiety, Popularity, and Happiness and Satisfaction. These scales presumably represent areas of importance to most respondents, warranting their inclusion in an overall self-evaluation scale.

Piers states her rationale as follows: "[The phenomenological] self-concept, as assessed by this instrument, is defined as a relatively stable set of self-attitudes reflecting both a description and an evaluation of one's own behavior and attributes" (Piers, 1984, p. 1). The self-concept has both global and specific components, and the "importance of each area [to the person] determines the degree to which success and failure affect overall self-evaluation" (Piers, 1984, p. 43).

Piers sees her views as being similar to the ideas of Shavelson, Hubner, and Stanton (1976) about the hierarchical, multi-faceted self. Also, she agrees with Dickstein (1977) and Harter (1978) that the importance of various self-concept facets to the individual determines the degree to which they affect overall self-regard. Nevertheless, the scale does not purport to determine the total score by summing a *weighted* combination of facets, but rather entails simple summation.

Item/Scale Selection and Refinement

From essays written by 2,893 children on the topics "What I Like About Myself" and "What I Dislike About Myself," Jersild (1952) inductively developed categories that yielded 90% intercoder reliability. The original 164 PH items were written to reflect Jersild's various categories of self-concept: physical characteristics and appearance, clothing and grooming, health and physical well-being, home and family, enjoyment and recreation, ability in sports and play, academic performance and attitudes toward school, intellectual abilities, special talents (music, arts), "just me myself," personality characteristics, inner resources, and emotional tendencies. However, Piers's categories do not exactly cover those of Jersild. She says her item factor analyses cut across some, but not all, of Jersild's areas.

"Double negatives and ambiguously worded items were avoided as were items with qualifiers such as 'many, often, or rarely,' which are subject to various interpretations" (Piers, 1984, p. 44). About half the items are negatively worded, half positively worded. Although Lie scale items were originally included, they were dropped when it was shown they did not contribute to scale validity. The item pool was culled by eliminating (1) most of those answered in the same direction by fewer than 10% or more than 90% of a preliminary sample of 90 children in grades 3, 4, and 5; (2) those that did not significantly discriminate between high and low total scorers in a sample of 127 sixth graders; and (3) those answered in the unexpected direction by more than half of the latter sample.

In contrast to Harter (1982) and Marsh (Marsh, Smith, & Barnes, 1983), Piers did not choose items originally with the hope of verifying the factorial distinctness of a priori clusters of items. Instead, she examined six item-level factor analyses of the PH and retained in the clusters only those items that were replicated across all these studies. Some items were not in any cluster scale but were nonetheless included in the total score. (These factor-analytic studies are considered below under Construct Validity.) The clusters are Behavior, Intellectual and School Status, Physical Appearance and Attributes, Anxiety, Popularity, and Happiness and Satisfaction.

There is item overlap between clusters that can have methodological implications for further studies that use them.

Samples

The original standardization sample consisted of 1,183 children in grades 4–12 in one Pennsylvania school district. Since that time, the PH scale has been used with a very large number of samples differing in age, gender, ethnicity, socioeconomic level, intellectual ability, nationality, health, and psychiatric status, and the test has been found appropriate for a wide variety of subjects. It is impractical to describe each sample here. Piers's (1984) manual gives details about her own samples and those used by others.

Descriptive Statistics

Piers (1984) gives total-score means for each of 17 samples and total-score standard deviations for 11 of them. The total N for these samples is 3,182. The amount of variation across samples should arouse appropriate cautions for both researchers and clinicians, since they cannot evaluate their scores or means with reference to those from any one published sample.

The score distributions are negatively skewed, as is the case with all self-evaluation instruments, so far as I know.

Piers (1984) also gives means and standard deviations for cluster scores, based on one sample of 485 children.

Reliability

Internal Consistency Coefficients for Total Scores
Piers (1984) gives 10 internal consistency coefficients, each based on a different sample. Values range from .88 to .93. The samples include 1,047 subjects, ages 6–14 years, grades 3–10.

Test-Retest Coefficients for Total Scores
Piers (1984) gives 19 test-retest reliabilities, each on a different sample. (Total $N = 1,577$ subjects, ages 6–16 years, grades 3–8, representing various ethnic groups.) Retest intervals ranged from 14 days to 1 year, and values of r range from .42 to .96 (median r = .75).

Piers (1984) cautions that despite high test-retest rs, there typically are increases in mean as large as five points, which reemphasizes the need for control observations.

Internal Consistency Coefficients for Cluster Scores
Based on the standardization sample for the cluster scales ($N = 582$), the alpha values for scales are Behavior, .81; Intellectual and School Status, .78; Physical Appearance and Attributes, .76; Anxiety, .77; Popularity, .74; Happiness and Satisfaction, .73. These values are obviously lower than those Marsh and his colleagues obtained for their factor scores. (See the review of the SDQ in this book.) Perhaps the difference originates from the fact that Marsh and his associates selected each item in a way intended to reflect one and only one of their a priori aspect dimensions, whereas the preparation of factorially distinct subscales was not a consideration in assembling items for the PH scale.

Test-Retest Coefficients for Cluster Scores
I found no information on this point.

Construct Validity

Factor-Analytic Checks on Dimensionality
Unlike Marsh and his colleagues (Marsh, Smith, & Barnes, 1983) and Harter (1982), Piers did not aim to choose subsets of items that would discriminantly measure different aspects of self-concept. Only after the PH was built did she and others factor analyze the interitem correlations.

The manual (Piers, 1984) reports the results from factoring 11 matrices and summarizes the outcomes as follows:

Four of the studies [seven matrices] (Michael, Smith, and Michael, 1975; Piers, 1973 [cited in Piers, 1984]; Rich, Barcikowski, and Witmer, 1979; Wolf, Sklov, Hunter, Webber, and Berenson, 1982) have replicated many or all of the factors identified in the original analysis (Piers, 1963) [cited in Piers, 1984]. The findings that roughly these same factors also replicate across different racial and ethnic minorities (Wolf et al., 1982), for differing age groups (Michael et al., 1975), and even on a sample of mentally retarded students (Rich et al., 1979), increases the credibility of these factors. However, many of the studies have identified additional factors or failed to replicate all six original factors. Even more disturbing is the work of Platten and Williams (1979, 1981) which identified factor instability within the same sample. . . . Obviously, additional research concerning the underlying dimensions of the *Piers-Harris* is still needed. (p. 66)

Nevertheless, cluster scales were set up on the basis of "several factor analyses." Some items are included in more than one scale, and some are not in any scale, albeit contributing to the total score.

No confirmatory factor analyses have been performed to test formally the possible invariance of one or more multidimensional factor patterns across groups differing in age, sex, nationality, ability, and so on.

Regarding the possible unidimensionality of the scale, Bentler (1972, p. 306) has pointed out that "a principal components analysis of binary [dichotomously scored] items such as those used in the [PH] scale tends to result in too many, and some spurious factors, as compared to a more appropriate procedure such as that of a monotonicity analysis." Thus the possible unidimensionality of the scale cannot be satisfactorily evaluated.

However, four sets of findings taken together suggest that the PH may be more unidimensional than multidimensional: (1) Correlations between items and total score range from .13 to .32. (2) Intercorrelations among the six cluster scores are substantial, ranging from .21 to .59, all significant at $p \leq .01$ (Piers, 1984), and from .43 to 1.00 in Winne, Marx, and Taylor's (1977) analysis. Of course the overlapping of items between scales contributes to these correlations. (3) Platten and Williams (1979, 1981) found that a disproportionately large amount of variance was accounted for by the first unrotated dimension in both their matrices. (4) As explained in the section below on multitrait-multimethod matrices, Winne, Marx, and Taylor (1977) found that subscale convergent validities were strong, but their discriminant validities were questionable or seriously deficient.

Irrelevant Response/Score Determiners
The following, with their attendant threats to validity, were avoided: forced-choice format, ipsative scoring, two-part indices (discrepancy scores), use of items keyed all in the positive or all in the negative direction, and items having double-negative or otherwise ambiguous wording. If dichotomous scoring is used, the remainder variance (as opposed to person and item variance) is artifactually inflated compared with what is obtainable with multistep scoring (Fiske, 1966). Also, limitations are set on the magnitudes of obtainable phi and Pearson r coefficients, depending on the item marginal splits. This can lead to possibly misleading results, as explained, for example, by Block (1965).

Social desirability. The use of a Lie scale to control for social desirability response set was tried, but it was dropped when it failed to affect validity.

Inconsistency scale. A computer-generated Inconsistency scale was developed to evaluate the prevalence of random responding as indicated by contradictory answers for paired items.

Item overlap. The overlap of items between subscales reduces the clarity of interpretation of subscale scores.

Low self-esteem scores from unreliable responding. Piers (1984) considered whether "low self-esteem" scores might often reflect unreliability of responding as opposed to poor self-esteem. This possibility arises because most scores fall in the upper scale range. Accordingly, a relatively low "self-esteem" score could be obtained by random responding due to guessing, misunderstanding, inability to read, or lack of cooperativeness. In the case of the PH scale with its dichotomous answers, random responding would tend to produce scores around 40.

Smith and Rogers (1977) attempted to evaluate this possible influence on PH scores by showing negligible mean total score change on retest for an originally high group; a mean change of +4.4 for the originally middle group; and a mean change of +8.4 for the originally low group. Although 8.4 was larger than 4.4

(which might indicate more unreliability in lower scores), the two means did not differ significantly; therefore Smith and Rogers (1977) believed they could rule out unreliability of responding as a possibly irrelevant determiner for low scores.

Convergent and Discriminant Validity

Multitrait-multimethod matrices. Winne, Marx, and Taylor (1977) analyzed intercorrelations of scores from similarly labeled scales of the PH scale, Gordon's "How I See Myself" scale, and the Sears Self-Concept Inventory. The authors conclude that the physical attribute subscales show strong convergent validity but very questionable discriminant validity. For the most part, convergent validity coefficients of subscales pertaining to social interaction are not strong, and the discriminant validity of these subscales "seems seriously deficient." The convergent validities of the academic subscales seem strong, but the discriminant validities are once again questionable.

There are no appropriate multitrait-multimethod analyses to help in evaluating the convergent and discriminant validity of the PH total scores. At the end of this section I compare information gotten from many different samples regarding reliability coefficients (both internal consistency and test-retest); convergent validity coefficients, involving alternate self-report tests of self-concept and self-concepts of respondents as rated by others; and correlations between PH self-concept reports and other self-report instruments purporting to measure other variables. (No information comparable to heterotrait-heteromethod *r*s is available.)

Such comparisons, based on widely disparate samples and procedures, are suggestive, but they obviously cannot serve in place of properly executed multitrait-multimethod analyses.

Convergence with other self-report scores of self-concept. One kind of convergent validity coefficient involves correlating PH scores with scores from other self-report instruments that also purport to measure "total self-concept" or "self-esteem." Eighteen such correlations based on a total of 2,629 subjects are given below. The mean *r* is .59, the range is .32 to .45.

Bills Index of Adjustment and Values	.42 and .40
Yonker, Blixt, and Dinero (1974)	
Bledsoe Self-Concept Scale	.37
Cowan, Altmann, and Pysh (1978)	
Children's Personality Questionnaire (o Factor)	.34 to .73
Karnes and Wherry (1982)	
Coopersmith Self-Esteem Inventory	
Johnson, Redfield, Miller, and Simpson (1983)	.63
Schauer (1975)	.85
Franklin, Duley, Rousseau, and Sabers (1981)	.78
Cowan, Altmann, and Pysh (1978)	.75
Lipsitt Self-Concept Scale for Children	.68
Mayer (1965)	
Personal Attributes Inventory for Children	
Parish and Taylor (1978a)	.67
Parish and Taylor (1978b)	.32
Purdue Self-Concept Scale	.51
Cowan, Altmann, and Pysh (1978)	
Pictorial Self-Concept Scale	.42
Bolea, Felker, and Barnes (1971)	
Tennessee Self-Concept Scale	
Yonker, Blixt, and Dinero (1974)	.51 and .61
Shavelson and Bolus (1982)	.80 at test, .73 at 4-month retest

Note that three out of the four highest correlations are with Coopersmith's Self-Esteem Inventory, which has a rationale, question format, and target age similar to those of the PH.

Although PH total scores purport to be overall self-esteem scores, I have not located any correlations between PH total scores and any "global self-esteem measure" such as the Rosenberg Self-Esteem Scale or the Rosenberg-Simmons Self-Esteem Scale (both reviewed in this book). If Piers's rationale is correct, these correlations should be substantial.

Convergence with inferred self-concept scores. Marsh and his colleagues (Marsh, Smith, & Barnes, 1983) have questioned whether correlations between self-reported self-concepts, especially those of similar content and format, may amount to alternate-form reliability coefficients rather than being validity coefficients. Accordingly they argue that, even though only the self-report respondents can have direct knowledge of their own self-conceptions, perceptive others who know them well can make valid inferences about their self-concepts. This implies that such inferred self-concept scores may constitute more appropriate convergent validity criteria for self-report indices of self-concept.

In her manual, Piers (1984) cites several unpublished studies of this kind, yielding the following results (total $N = 548$):

Teacher ratings of self-concept	(* $p < .05$, ** $p < .01$)
Piers (1965)	.06, .17, .25, .41**
Mettes (1974)	.55**
Querry (1970)	.02, .26, .54**
Peer ratings of self-concept	(* $p < .05$, ** $p < .01$)
Piers (1965)	.26, .34*, .41**, .49**

No information is published about the tools or instructions involved in either teacher or peer rating procedures or on whether interrater differences in general use of the scales may have been statistically accounted for.

Parenthetically, it is interesting that the mean of the eight rs involving teacher rating (.38) is essentially comparable to the mean convergent validity coefficient from seven multitrait-multimethod matrices reported by Marsh and his colleagues, also using teacher ratings of inferred self-concept (.34). (For details, see the review of the SDQ in this book.) In comparing SDQ and PH results, one should note that the latter concern total inferred self-concept (self-esteem), whereas the former concern inferences regarding various factorially determined facets of self-concept.

Discriminant validity of the total score. Correlations with self-report scales that purport to measure variables other than self-esteem may throw some light on the discriminant validity of PH self-esteem scores, and the findings are also relevant to another validity question considered below: Are PH self-concept scores related to other variables in a manner consistent with theory?

Six correlations between the Children's Manifest Anxiety Scale and total PH scores ranging from $-.54$ to $-.69$ are reported by Millen (1966) and by Cowan, Altmann, and Pysh (1978). These may be large partly because the PH contains an Anxiety scale.

Six correlations with the Children's Social Desirability Scale ranging from .31 to .42 are reported by Millen (1966) and by Cowan, Altmann, and Pysh (1978).

Tavormina (1975) and Chapman (1973, cited in Piers, 1984) both report negative correlations with Neuroticism (−.47, −.27) and positive correlations with Extraversion (.40, .41) from the Junior Eysenck Personality Questionnaire. (Chapman used 455 English children, aged 10–11 years.)

Rotundo and Hensley (1985) report $r = -.87$ between PH scores and the Children's Depression Scale (which includes a self-esteem scale). Additionally, Saylor, Finch, Baskin, Furey, and Kelly (1984) report a correlation of −.64 between the PH and the Children's Depression Inventory, and Strauss, Forehand, Frame, and Smith (1984) found significant differences in PH scores between high and low scorers on this inventory.

Using the SRA Junior Inventory, Cox (1966) obtained a correlation of −.64 between the PH and "big problems" and −.48 between the PH and "problems related to health."

Felker and Thomas (1971) and Piers (1977) report correlations of .32 and .35 between PH total scores and self-attributions of success on the Intellectual Achievement Responsibility Questionnaire (IAR).

Brunn (1975), as reported by Piers (1984), found that "[total] self-concept and body cathexis are closely related constructs, with body cathexis most closely related to the Physical Appearance and Attributions Scale" (p. 62).

Wheeler and Ladd (1982) found a significant r of .36 between PH total scores and their newly devised Children's Self-Efficacy for Peer Interaction Scale.

In summary, the magnitudes of reliability and convergent validity coefficients for total scores fall in the order listed from (1) to (3) below. This order is consonant with expectations concerning reliability and validity coefficients.

(1) Internal consistency reliability coefficients, mean r from 10 samples is .90 (range .88 to .93). (2) Test-retest reliability coefficients, mean r from 20 samples is .75 (range .42 to .96). (3) Convergent validity coefficients involving (a) another self-report

measure purported to index overall self-concept, mean *r* from 18 samples, 6 different tests, is .59 (range .32 to .85); (b) teachers' or peers' inferences about respondents' self-concepts, mean *r* from 8 teacher samples is .38 (range .02 to .54), mean *r* from 4 peer samples is .38 (range .26 to .49). This trend seems reasonable. But when we examine some of the correlations between total PH scores and self-report instruments purporting to measure non-self-concept variables (where one would hope to find still lower *r*s if PH scores have discriminant validity), we actually find disappointingly large coefficients, for example, with self-reports of anxiety, body cathexis, depression, extraversion, locus of control, and neuroticism. The relative magnitudes of these *r*s compared with validity coefficients for PH total scores casts doubt on the discriminant validity of the total PH scores.

Assumed Validity Studies
In addition to studies of the type considered immediately above, the following are also relevant to validity evaluations, since they explore the relations between assumedly valid PH scores and other variables to which these scores might plausibly be related.

Intellectual variables. Because Intellectual and School Status is one of the six revised cluster scales for the PH, one might expect some positive correlation, albeit moderate, between PH total scores and intellectual variables such as achievement tests and ability indicators.

Eight studies based on 1,785 subjects from grades 3–6 yielded correlations of PH total scores with a variety of *achievement tests* and *grade point averages,* ranging from .02 to .57, almost all significant at $p \leq .001$. The studies are reported by Black (1974), Davis, Dokecki, Coleman, Smith, and Wood (cited in Piers, 1984), Hughes (1971), McIntire and Drummond (1977), Piers (1965, cited in Piers, 1984), Piers (1973, cited in Piers, 1984), Piers and Harris (1964), Schauer (1975), and Smith, Zingale, and Coleman (1978) (where differences within high SES but not low SES groups were found).

Two studies examined the relation of *achievement* to both PH total scores and separate cluster scores. Only the Intellectual and

School Status scale significantly differentiated achievers from underachievers (Kanoy, Johnson, & Kanoy, 1980). Reck (1980) found no significant relation between achievement and the total score or between achievement and any of the six cluster scales. By contrast, of 21 correlations between total self-concept scores and various IQ scores, only 6 were significant. (Total N from nine studies = 1,279, from grades 3–10 [Black, 1974; Cox, 1966; Drummond, 1977; Eastman, 1965, cited in Piers, 1984; Mayer, 1965; McIntire & Drummond, 1977; Piers, 1965, Piers, 1973, cited in Piers, 1984; Piers & Harris, 1964; Schauer, 1975].)

One would expect the intellectual variables to correlate more highly with the Intellectual and School Status cluster score than with the PH total score. The only three available correlations involving IQ are .43, .50, .44, which exceed all but one of the correlations between PH total scores and IQ scores (Eastman, 1965, cited in Piers, 1984; Davis, Dokecki, Coleman, Smith, & Wood, 1975). (Total N = 242.) Davis et al. also obtained a correlation of .53 between *mathematics achievement scores* and Intellectual and School Status scores.

Sheare (1978) reported that learning-disabled children had lower PH scores than normals at two testing times.

Interventions. Learning-disabled children who received 6 months of special treatment from a "modulator" showed no more increase in PH scores than did an untreated control group (Pihl, Parkes, Drake, & Vrana, 1980).

Sex differences. The numerous researches looking for sex differences in PH total scores are not, strictly speaking, "assumed validity" studies, since, although previous failure to obtain sex differences in self-esteem was noted (Wylie, 1974), no theoretical predictions were tested. Moreover, no confirmatory analyses of factorial invariance across gender are at hand as a background for interpreting any sex mean differences.

Nevertheless, it is interesting that 11 data sets failed to show sex differences in PH total scores: Crase, Foss, and Colbert (1981), DeVoe (1977), Farls (1966), cited in Piers (1984), Kanoy, Johnson, and Kanoy (1980), Ketcham and Snyder (1977), Lord

(1971), Millen (1966), Moyal (1977), Osborne and LeGette (1982), Piers (1965, cited in Piers, 1984), and Piers and Harris (1964).

These studies included more than 2,700 subjects, grades 9–12. Only Stopper (1978) found gifted females' total scores exceeding those of gifted males (grades 2, 4, 6), and McIntire and Drummond (1977), in a multiple regression study, found that sex accounted for only 1.4% of the variance.

Age differences. Although the studies reviewed in Wylie (1979) did not support an association between age and self-concept scores, some writers have suggested that at least certain self-conceptions may reasonably be expected to remain stable in elementary school, decline during early adolescence, and rise again in later adolescence and early adulthood. (See, for example, Bachman & O'Malley, 1977; Marsh, in press b; Simmons, Rosenberg, & Rosenberg, 1973.)

Clearly interpretable age data relevant to these speculations are not at hand for PH total scores or cluster scores. For one thing, factorial invariance across age groups has not been explored as a basis of interpreting any mean PH age effects. Second, the age range covered in any one study is often narrow. And of course cross-sectional data are not the most suitable basis for longitudinal conclusions.

In any case, data from the standardization group (1,183 students from grades 4, 6, 8, 10, and 12) yielded no age effects (Piers, 1984). Data from 15 other sources covering narrow age ranges also yielded null findings (Piers, 1984).

The question whether these null trends reflect on the construct validity of PH scores or on the plausibility of theoretical predictions about age effects is, of course, moot.

Personality characteristics. Rotundo and Hensley (1985) found significant differences in PH total scores between clinically depressed children and normal children.

Guiton and Zachary (1984), using elementary, junior-high and senior-high pupils, found a significant mean difference between a "clinical" sample and a "normal group."

Cox (1966) reports four correlations (.31 to .43) between

PH scores and teacher and peer ratings of "socially effective behavior" and "ego strength."

Guyot, Fairchild, and Johnson (1984) partially confirmed Witkin's prediction that "field independent" persons should have higher self-esteem. The correlation of PH scores with scores from a modified Embedded Figures Test was significant for girls but not for boys. Hoffman (1976), cited in Guyot, Fairchild, and Johnson (1984), obtained a significant relation between field independence and PH scores for boys.

Partly supporting their prediction, Elkind and Bowen (1979) found the PH total scores significantly more highly correlated with their self-made "Abiding Self" scale (−.32) than with their self-made "Transient Self" scale (−.16).

Mannarino (1978) reported significantly higher PH scores among preadolescent males who were more involved in "chum" relationships than in those who were less involved.

Parental practices and attitudes. In a multiple-correlation analysis involving family background and social variables and parental child-rearing practices and attitudes, Cox (1966) found that 72% of the predicted variance in self-concept was associated with child-rearing practices.

The studies mentioned above have explored whether PH total scores are associated with a variety of other variables in ways that might be predicted by "theory." Taken together, these studies support a range of intuitive, though not rigorously theoretical, predictions.

The least interpretable are those using a self-report measure of the variable being related to the PH. Somewhat more interpretable are those relating the PH to another variable measured by means other than self-report. However, all the studies have limited value in supporting the validity of PH total scores because, as is always the case, this general approach gives at best the most ambiguous source of support; theory is not always stated clearly; sources of artifact are often present; and predicted results are not always found.

(Readers may wish to look at the following reviews of the PH: Jeske, 1985; Epstein, 1985; and Bentler, 1972.)

Sample Items from the Piers-Harris Children's Self-Concept Scale

I often get into trouble. (Behavior)

I can give a good report in front of the class. (Intellectual and School Status)

I am strong. (Physical Appearance and Attributes)

I worry a lot. (Anxiety)

I have many friends. (Popularity)

I am a happy person. (Happiness and Satisfaction)

3

ROSENBERG SELF-ESTEEM
SCALE (RSE)
(Rosenberg, 1965)

Rationale and General Description

Each of the 10 items in this instrument is intended to measure "global self-esteem" in the sense described by Rosenberg (1979):

When we characterize a person as having high self-esteem . . . we mean that he has self-respect, considers himself a person of worth. Appreciating his own merits, he nonetheless recognizes his faults . . . that he hopes and expects to overcome. . . . The term "low self-esteem" . . . means that the individual lacks respect for himself, considers himself unworthy, inadequate, or otherwise seriously deficient as a person. (p. 54)

. . . the self-concept is not a *collection* but an organization of parts, pieces, and components, and . . . these are hierarchically organized and interrelated in complex ways. (p. 73)

[Global self-attitude and parts of the self-concept] are not identical or interchangeable: both exist within the individual's phenomenal field as separate and distinguishable entities, and each can and should be studied in its own right. (p. 20)

Although many researchers attempt to get a global self-esteem index by summing across scores for items of disparate content, this is obviously not Rosenberg's idea of the appropriate approach. In his view, one cannot safely make assumptions about which specific content areas to tap or how to evaluate the relative importance of each to the self-esteem of various respondents.

Accordingly, he has taken the "direct approach" to item writing, assuming that each individual, in developing his or her global self-esteem, has consciously and/or unconsciously taken into account and weighted a unique set of attributes of varying personal importance.

Item/Scale Selection and Refinement

The 10 items were written and scaled taking into account the desiderata of ease of administration, economy of time, unidimensionality, and face validity. Answers to each could range from Strongly Agree to Strongly Disagree (Rosenberg, 1965).

Partly because of the desire for unidimensionality, the items were set up as a Guttman scale comprising 7 "contrived items," but most researchers use the simpler method of summing across the 10 items, scoring disagreements with negative items positively. In this approach, an individual's score could range from 0 to 40 if all four steps on each Likert scale are used, or from 0 to 10 with dichotomous scoring of each item.

I found no mention of a preliminary pool of items from which these were drawn according to any psychometric criteria. Several studies, many of them large scale, are based on only a subgroup of the 10 items, and selection criteria are not always mentioned (e.g., Bachman, 1970; Kohn, 1969). This is regrettable from the standpoint of interstudy comparisons and relevance of outcomes to evaluating the validity of the 10-item RSE.

Samples

The scale was first used in Rosenberg's 1965 study of 5,024 students from 10 high schools chosen randomly from all New York State high schools, stratified by size of community.

No subsequent samples were used for purposes of scale development, but the scale and its modifications have been widely used in substantive research studies, with a range of nationalities, ages, socioeconomic levels, ethnicity, and psychiatric conditions, as exemplified in later sections of this review.

Descriptive Statistics

The Guttman-scale version of the RSE yields scores from 0 to 6, with a mean of 1.89, standard deviation of 1.44, and skewness of .648. When subjects were divided into high, medium, and low self-esteem for analyses involving other variables, high self-esteem = 0 and 1 (44.8% of subjects); medium self-esteem = 2 (25.1% of subjects); and low self-esteem = 3–6 (30.0% of subjects). This information is based on 1,583 New York State high-school students (M. Rosenberg, personal communication, April 22, 1987).

That 44.8% of the subjects' scale scores fell in the two highest of the seven steps of the scale gives an alternate indication that the distribution of responses was quite skewed.

No descriptive statistics are available for the Likert-scale scoring of the 10 RSE statements, although several researchers have used the RSE with large samples—for example, Byrne and Shavelson (1986), $N = 991$; Dobson, Goudy, Keith, and Powers (1979), $N = 1,332$; Hensley (1977), $N = 1,194$; Schmitt and Bedeian (1982), $N = 873$. Had these reports included such information, it could be useful as a basis for evaluating scores against the "norms" from a suitable reference group, or perhaps from the entire pool of subjects if descriptive statistics turned out to be comparable across groups.

Reliability

Internal Consistency
For the New York State sample, Cronbach alpha was .77. Also, for these subjects and about 560 British adolescents, the Coefficients of Reproducibility for Guttman-scale scores were respectively .92 and "slightly higher" (M. Rosenberg, 1965, and personal communication, April 22, 1987). The minimum Coefficient of Reproducibility for satisfactory reliability is usually taken to be at least .90.

At least seven alpha coefficients for the 10-item scores are reported: Schmitt and Bedeian (1982), 873 civil servants, .83; Orme, Reis, and Herz (1986), 116 parents, .80; Dobson, Goudy,

Keith, and Powers (1979), 1,332 men 60 years old or older, .72; and Ward (1977), 323 noninstitutionalized persons 60 years old or older, .74. Byrne and Shavelson (1986) report alpha coefficients of .87 for 832 urban Canadian 11th and 12th graders: .87 for 420 females, and .74 for 412 males.

Test-Retest
I have found only two test-retest coefficients: Silber and Tippett (1965), 2-week interval, 28 college students, .85; and Byrne (1983), 7-month interval, 990 urban Canadian high-school students, .63. Without stating a time interval, Shorkey and Whiteman (1978) say they obtained an *r* of .91 when a Spanish (or English) version was given first and the opposite-language version was given later.

Alternate Forms
From her application of facet analysis to the RSE, Dancer (1985) has proposed a systematic way to go about creating additional, very general "content free" scales with different wording. This approach could provide a useful alternate form of the RSE with testable levels of alternate-form reliability.

Construct Validity

Guttman and Factor-Analytic Checks on Dimensionality
Rosenberg's interest in demonstrating Guttman scalability of his items was to test his assumption that his scale was unidimensional.

When the items have face validity for measuring the intended construct, a Coefficient of Reproducibility of .90 or more is taken as an arbitrary minimum for inferring unidimensionality (although successful Guttman scaling does not guarantee unidimensionality in such a case). As already indicated, Rosenberg's Coefficients of Reproducibility were .92 or more.

Other findings that might suggest unidimensionality are the two matrices of item intercorrelations published by Carmines and Zeller (1979) and by McIver and Carmines (1981), the latter cited by Dancer (1985). The respective sets of correlation values run from .045 to .577 and from .134 to .509. Interestingly, the *r*s involving the item "I wish I could have more respect for myself" are lower than almost all other values in the matrices.

Results of eight factor analyses vary, some being unidimensional, some two-factor solutions.

O'Brien (1985) reported strong support for unidimensionality. A single factor with an eigenvalue of 5.28 accounted for 52.8% of the variance, and no other factor had an eigenvalue of 1.00 or more. Factor loadings for the 10 items range from .57 to .81.

Hensley (1977) also obtained a one-factor solution in both his male (*N* = 487) and female (*N* = 707) samples, all college students. Interestingly, all positively worded items had positive loadings and all negatively worded ones had negative loadings.

Each of five other factor analyses yielded a two-factor solution: Kohn (1969) (based on only six items), 3,000 males 16 years old or older; Kaplan and Pokorny (1969), 500 adults of all ages; Hensley and Roberts (1976), 479 university students; Dobson, Goudy, Keith, and Powers (1979), 1,322 men 60 years old or older; and Carmines and Zeller (1979), 340 high-school students.

There is considerable agreement concerning which items define the respective factors: all five studies agree on five items, and four of the five agree on two other items. Even the suggested names agree to some extent; for example, self-derogation, negative self-esteem, self-depreciation for one factor, and conventional defense of self-worth, self-confidence, and positive self-esteem for the other.

In support of discriminant validity for the two factors, Kaplan and Pokorny (1969) found that items weighted according to their association with Factor I (self-derogation) correlated with a range of other variables, whereas items weighted according to their association with Factor II (conventional defense of self-worth) did not.

Despite this evidence for two factors, Hensley and Roberts (1976) and Carmines and Zeller (1979) believe that their two factors represent some kind of "response set" and that the scale is basically unidimensional. For one thing, Hensley and Roberts (1976), Hensley (1977), and Carmines and Zeller (1979) all present evidence that either the direction of item loadings on a general factor (Hensley, 1977) or the allocation of items to two factors cleanly separates the items into those that are worded self-favorably and self-unfavorably. In Dancer's (1985) facet analysis of McIver and Carmines's (1981) matrix, positive versus negative wording turned out to be what she called a "format facet." (McIver and Carmines used 943 subjects from Rosenberg's 1965 sample from New York State.)

In addition, Carmines and Zeller (1979), differing from Kaplan and Pokorny (1969), got amazingly similar correlations between each of their two RSE factors and a range of variables. This supported their idea that the RSE represents a single psychological construct, since no discriminant validity for the two factors was obtained.

Hensley (1977) reports that his one-factor solution was "quite similar" for 487 college males and 707 college females (average difference in factor loadings = .058). However, I have found no formal explorations of factorial invariance across gender, age, or nationality groups.

Irrelevant Response/Score Determiners
The following, with their attendant threats to validity, were avoided: item ambiguity, forced-choice format, ipsative scoring, and two-part indices (discrepancy scores). (It is assumed that "discrepancies" between self and ideal, for example, have been taken into account by the respondent when answering each item.)

Because scale scores are so skewed, "low self-esteem" scores are close to the numerical center of the scale, which raises the question whether such scores validly indicate low self-esteem or may come from random responding due to lack of cooperation or attention, poor reading ability, and so on. This problem could lessen the interpretability of any differences obtained between groups differing in ability, reading skills, ethnicity, socioeconomic level, or clinical diagnosis.

Half the items are positively worded, half negatively worded to control for acquiescent response set.

No attempt is made to disguise the social-desirability level of items or to take account of possible social-desirability "faking" by any kind of correction scheme. Rather, it is assumed that subjects will honestly report their phenomenal self-esteem if they are given anonymity (as in Rosenberg's 1965 study) or if they are especially motivated to be cooperative (e.g., Silber and Tippett's 1965 research).

Convergent and Discriminant Validity
Multitrait-multimethod matrices. I found three multitrait-multimethod matrices involving the RSE. The earliest one, by Silber and Tippett (1965), involves a problem in that the Heath and the Kelly Repertory tests were each used to define two variables (self-image stability and self-esteem).

At each of two times, Byrne (1983) intercorrelated the RSE with Coopersmith's Self-Esteem Inventory, Coopersmith's School-Academic subscale, and Brookover's Self-Concept of Ability Scale (Coopersmith, 1981; Brookover, 1962). In each matrix, the convergent validity coefficient for self-esteem exceeded all other correlations in the matrix. In the Time 1 matrix, the convergent validity coefficient was .58, while other rs ranged from .35 to .46. In the Time 2 matrix, the convergent validity coefficient was .60, while other rs ranged from .37 to .42. ($N = 992$ urban Canadian 9th to 12th graders.)

Byrne and Shavelson (1986) present a multitrait-multimethod matrix with three measures of general academic self-concept, three measures of mathematics self-concept, three measures of English self-concept, and the following three measures of "general self-concept" (self-esteem): the RSE, the Self-Concept subscale of the API (Soares & Soares, 1979), and the General Self (Esteem) scale of the SDQ III (which is based on the RSE and Bachman's modification of it (Marsh & O'Neill, 1984). For the RSE, convergent validity coefficients were .79 with the General Self-Concept of SDQ III and .64 with the Self-Concept subscale of the API. These correlations exceeded all heterotrait-monomethod and heterotrait-heterotrait correlations in the matrix, indicative of discriminant as well as convergent validity.

(*N* = 516 males and 475 females, urban Canadians in grades 11 and 12.)

Convergent validity coefficients. In addition to the convergent validity coefficients just reported are the following. Rosenberg and Simmons (1972) mention a gamma of .6119 between a seven-item version of the RSE and their general self-esteem scale for elementary- and secondary-school children (Rosenberg and Simmons Self-Esteem Scale). Respondents were secondary-school students.

Silber and Tippett (1965) report correlations of .67 with the Kelly Repertory Test sum of self-minus-ideal discrepancies, .83 with Heath's Self-Image Questionnaire, and .56 with interviewers' ratings of self-esteem (*N* = 24 college students).

Demo (1985) obtained *r*s of .55 and .65 with the Coopersmith Self-Esteem Inventory. Demo (1985) also correlated the RSE with other purported tests of self-esteem, with the following results: peer rating of respondents' self-regard, *r* = .32; observer checklist of behaviors allegedly indicative of self-regard, *r*s = .15 and .12 (n.s.); observer *Q*-sort (Block) inferring respondents' self-regard, .19 (n.s.) and .45; interview to infer respondents' self-regard, .42 (this was actually an oral presentation of some Likert-type scales); "beeper method," *r* = .20. All but the Block *Q*-sort are idiosyncratic instruments devised or modified by the author. In the absence of more psychometric information about these measures, the small validity coefficients cannot be evaluated as indicating poor validity of the RSE.

O'Brien (1985) correlated the RSE with the total score from Eagly's revision of the Janis-Field Feelings of Inadequacy Scale (*r* = .82) and with four separate factors derived from that scale. For two general evaluation factors, *r*s = .74 and .71. For two "situationally limited" factors, *r*s = .45 and .48. This set of four correlations supports the validity of the RSE for measuring general self-esteem rather than specific aspects of self-regard.

From a scale they devised that yielded five factors, Fleming and Courtney (1984) found correlations between the factors and the RSE as follows: self-regard, .78, self-confidence, .51; school ability, .35; physical appearance, .42; physical ability, .35. Again, the pattern of correlations supports the validity of the RSE for measuring general self-regard rather than specific aspects.

Assumed Validity Studies
As already mentioned, this approach necessarily yields the most ambiguous support to the construct validity of any instrument. However, Rosenberg (1965, p. 18) justifies its use by saying:

Unfortunately, there are no "known groups" or "criterion groups" which can be used to validate the scale. The adequacy of the measure must thus be defended on the following grounds: if this scale actually did measure self-esteem, then we would expect the scores on this scale to be associated with other data in a theoretically meaningful way.

From his preliminary work, he then cites expectation-fulfilling associations between the RSE scores of 50 normal young-adult volunteers being studied in the National Institutes of Health and (1) likelihood of appearing "gloomy and disappointed" to the nurses on the ward; (2) likelihood of nurses' judging them as "well thought of," "makes good impression," "often admired, respected by others," "able to criticize self," and "touchy and easily hurt."

Regarding another kind of expectation-fulfilling result, Rosenberg found an association between RSE scores and number of choices as class leader ($N = 272$ high-school seniors).

Additional expectation-fulfilling associations from Rosenberg's (1965) New York State sample and from numerous more recent publications include the following:

Depressive affect. There are several reports of significant associations between self-reported depression and the RSE: Rosenberg (1965), using his Guttman Scale of Depressive Affect, significant chi-square; Gould (1982), using the Beck Depression Inventory, $r = .32$; Orme, Reis, and Herz (1986), using the Center for Epidemiological Studies Depression Scale (CES-D), $r = .31$. Additionally, using their self-derogation factor score, Kaplan and Pokorny (1969) found significant associations with the Rosenberg Scale of Depressive Affect.

Anxiety and psychosomatic symptoms. In the New York group (Rosenberg, 1965) and in Kaplan and Pokorny's (1969) study using a self-derogation score, a negative relation was obtained between the RSE and the number of psychosomatic symptoms reported. Orme, Reis, and Herz (1986) obtained *r*s of −.44 and −.46 with Spielberger's State and Trait Anxiety scores.

Clinical diagnosis. Harder, Strauss, Kokes, and Ritzler (1984), studying 152 psychiatric inpatients and 97 outpatients, found within each sample that a seven-item self-derogation score was significantly related to severity of diagnosis, overall health/sickness, and a measure of difficulty in social/employment aspects of life.

They say, "As predicted by the overall hypothesis, self-derogation relates significantly to the severity of pathology, however measured, in two different samples, independent of other potentially overlapping variables" (p. 234).

Kaplan (1978), also using a seven-item self-derogation score, found an association with "deviant behaviors" in middle-class but not lower-class junior-high-school subjects (*N* = 4,694). Based on a 2-year longitudinal design, self-derogation was said to be antecedent.

Interpersonal insecurity. Rosenberg's New York subjects with low RSE scores significantly more often reported themselves as having difficulty in making friends, being sensitive to criticism from others, being lonely, shy persons, and being bothered by others' poor opinion of them (Rosenberg, 1965).

When Ward (1977) used multiple regression to predict RSE scores among elderly persons, he found that the negativity of respondents' personal attitudes toward old people was the best predictor when other predictors included age-related deprivations, activity, health, age, education, and income.

In his study of loneliness, Hojat (1982) used a Farsi translation of the RSE and Iranian college students, 283 studying in the United States and 305 in Iran. The correlations between RSE scores and the UCLA Loneliness Scale are −.52 and −.43. Using four additional variables to predict Loneliness scores, he found that the RSE contributed significantly to predicting these scores in each group.

Parental lack of interest. A combined index of respondents' reports of parental lack of interest and lack of interest of other family members in what respondents said was significantly negatively associated with the RSE in Rosenberg's (1965) New York group.

Participation in activities; leadership. In Rosenberg's New York group, RSE scores were significantly associated with self-reported participation in such things as extracurricular activities, club memberships, elected positions, and discussions. In another group of 272 high-school seniors, subjects with high RSE scores were significantly more often nominated by peers as someone they would vote for as "leader of English class today" (Rosenberg, 1965).

In studies of creative problem-solving skills relevant to professional managers, Keller and Holland (1978) and Goldsmith (1985) found significant correlations between RSE scores and scores on the Kirton Adaption-Innovation Inventory, especially the Originality subscale.

Body esteem. Franzoi and Shields (1984) and Franzoi and Herzog (1986) correlated RSE scores with each of three subscales of their factor-analyzed Body Esteem Scale (reviewed in this book). For college females, rs were Sexual Attractiveness, .32, .21; Weight Concern, .19, .36; and Physical Condition, .35, .39. For college males, the values were Physical Attractiveness, .50, .26; Upper Body Strength, .45, .25; and Physical Condition, .51, .40. ($N = 194$ males, 171 females.) In their second study they used multiple regression to predict RSE scores from their three subscale scores, finding that 17.6% and 21.6% of the male and female variance in RSE scores was accounted for by these body-esteem factors.

Rationality. Whiteman (1979) and Whiteman and Shorkey (1978) report a correlation of .45 (in each study) between RSE scores and the Rational Behavior Inventory, Australian version and United States version. ($N = 74$ and 222 students.) (The Rational Behavior Inventory purports to be an index of rationality based on Ellis's rational-emotive therapy approach.)

Locus of control. In high, medium, and low socioeconomic level respondents, Guterman (1982) obtained rs of .24, .22, and .22 between RSE scores and a shortened version of Rotter's Locus-of-Control Scale. ($N = 2,213$ 10th-grade boys studied by Bachman, 1970.)

Conflict resolution. Because values-clarification proponents claim that high self-esteem is often an indicator of being clear about one's values, RSE scores were predicted to correlate positively with self-reported conflict-resolution scores on a new Values Conflict Resolution Assessment Scale. Results confirmed the prediction (Kinnier, 1987). ($N = 120$ graduate students in counseling, aged 21–55 years.)

Confidence and popularity. As predicted, two factors from a Self-Attitude Inventory correlated positively with the RSE: Confidence correlated .65 and .69 for two samples; Popularity (Social Approval) correlated .39 and .43 for the two samples (Lorr & Wunderlich, 1986). ($N = 214$ Catholic high-school boys.)

Despite the number and reasonableness of all the assumed validity findings reported above, caution is in order on two counts. (1) Most of the studies involved correlating two self-reports, leaving obvious but indeterminate possibilities for common method factors to influence outcomes in a direction favorable to the validity of the RSE. (2) Because many variables correlate with RSE, we need theoretical arguments for expected relative sizes of correlations of a wide variety of variables with RSE, and corresponding cross-validated multivariate analyses to try to confirm these expectations.

Items from the Rosenberg Self-Esteem Scale

Each item answered on a four-point scale from Strongly Agree to Strongly Disagree

1. I feel that I'm a person of worth, at least on an equal plane with others.
2. I feel that I have a number of good qualities.
3. All in all, I am inclined to feel that I am a failure.
4. I am able to do things as well as most other people.
5. I feel I do not have much to be proud of.
6. I take a positive attitude toward myself.
7. On the whole, I am satisfied with myself.
8. I wish I could have more respect for myself.
9. I certainly feel useless at times.
10. At times I think I am no good at all.

4

ROSENBERG-SIMMONS
SELF-ESTEEM SCALE (RSSE)
(Rosenberg & Simmons, 1972)

Rationale and General Description

Because Rosenberg and Simmons (1972) felt that the 10-item Rosenberg Self-Esteem Scale for adolescents was not suitably worded for use with respondents below high-school age, they constructed another, 6-item version for their large-scale study of the self-esteem of black and white children aged 8–19. Each item is scored dichotomously.

Their underlying rationale for this scale is the same as that used in construction of the Rosenberg Self-Esteem Scale (reviewed in this book). They believe that global self-worth (self-esteem) is a measurable, unidimensional phenomenological construct separate from, although influenced by, evaluations of specific aspects of self. The person of high self-esteem "considers himself a person of worth," has fundamental respect for self, and appreciates his own merits even though he is aware of faults in himself that he hopes and expects to overcome. He does "not necessarily consider himself better than most others." A person with low self-esteem is one who "lacks respect for himself, considers himself unworthy, inadequate, or otherwise seriously deficient as a person" (Rosenberg, 1979, p. 54).

Differing from those who purport to get a global self-esteem score by summing across the responses to an array of specific items of disparate content selected by the test maker, Rosenberg and Simmons (1972, p. 12) say, "In constructing our scale items, we sought to insure that [the items] dealt quite explicitly and overtly with the concept of self-esteem." In this way they hoped to have each respondent's self-esteem score reflect the idiosyncratic combination and weighting of the different aspects of self-concept that enter into global self-esteem.

Rather than expecting the children to read the self-esteem items, the authors presented the items as part of a long interview (Rosenberg & Simmons, 1972; Simmons, Brown, Bush, & Blyth, 1978).

Item/Scale Selection and Refinement

No information is given about any larger pool of face-valid items from which these items were selected or about any kind of empirical test used to cull items for the final form. Rosenberg and Simmons (1972, p. 11) say only that the scale "had been extensively pretested with children of different ages and from different social backgrounds."

Two of the items are worded positively and four negatively, and each is scored dichotomously.

Collectively the items constitute a Guttman scale for the Baltimore sample (Coefficient of Reproducibility, .902; Coefficient of Scalability, .676) (Rosenberg & Simmons, 1972), and for the Milwaukee sample (Coefficient of Reproducibility, .93; Coefficient of Scalability, .70) (Simmons, Brown, Bush, & Blyth, 1978). This suggests but does not demonstrate that the scale indexes a unidimensional construct, consonant with the authors' theoretical view about self-esteem.

Samples

The original sample included 1,917 children, grades 3–12, from public schools in the city of Baltimore; 64% were black, and they were "more heavily working class than the national average" (Simmons, Rosenberg, & Rosenberg, 1973, p. 555).

A second sample comprised 798 black and white children from a stratified sample of 18 schools in Milwaukee. The stratification variables were percentage of minority students and size of school. These subjects were followed from 6th to 7th grade. A subsample comprising 161 boys and 149 girls was followed from 7th through 10th grade.

These are sizable samples, chosen to be widely representative of racial and socioeconomic groups in two rather different cities. Thus far no rural subjects or special educational or clinical groups have been used in exploring the characteristics of this instrument.

Descriptive Statistics

Item means, total score means, item marginal splits, and indices of skew are not published. Dividing lines between high, medium, and low self-esteem are not specified, but Rosenberg (personal communication April 22, 1987) reports a strong negative skew.

Reliability

Internal Consistency
The usual reliability estimates for the RSSE are not given in Rosenberg and Simmons's (1972) book. The Coefficients of Reproducibility from the Guttman scaling of the Baltimore and Milwaukee samples reach or exceed the usually accepted minimum (.90) for acceptable reliability, with the same results being obtained for the blacks and whites in the Baltimore sample.

For the Milwaukee sample, alpha was .72 (Simmons & Blyth, 1987).

Test-Retest
For 161 boys and 149 girls who responded to the RSSE five times from grade 6 through grade 10, the average one-year test-retest correlation for both genders was .54. The correlations between tests in grades 6 and 7 were .46 for boys, .53 for girls, whereas the correlations between tests in grades 9 and 10 were .48 for boys and .61 for girls (Simmons & Blyth, 1987). The correlation between grade 6 and grade 10, both genders, was .36.

The trend in mean RSSE across time (grades 6–10) was

upward. For a four point-in-time repeated measures analysis, p < .0001 (Simmons & Blyth, 1987).

Construct Validity

Factor-Analytic Checks on Dimensionality
As mentioned above, for both the Baltimore and Milwaukee samples the items of the RSSE collectively constitute a Guttman scale. This suggests, but does not demonstrate, that the scale indexes a unidimensional construct, consonant with the authors' theoretical view about self-esteem.

Factor analysis shows the two positive items loading less highly on a general factor than do the four negative ones. However, Simmons reports "a chi-square goodness-of-fit measure for the self-esteem measurement model . . . indicates that the self-esteem scale is a one-factor model . . . and recent multivariate LISREL analyses run with only the four negative items are virtually the same as those run with all six items included" (R. Simmons, personal communication, July 20, 1987).

Irrelevant Response/Score Determiners
The following, with their attendant threats to validity, were avoided: forced-choice format, ipsative scoring, two-part indices (discrepancy scores), and item wording that is confusing or involves double negatives.

Dichotomous scoring. The use of dichotomous rather than multistep scoring promotes artifactual inflation of the remainder variance (as opposed to person and item variance) (Fiske, 1966). Also, depending on the item marginal splits, dichotomous scoring can set limits on obtainable phi coefficients and Pearson r coefficients, with possibly misleading results (Block, 1965). If a principal-components factor analysis were to be undertaken with these binary items, too many factors and some spurious ones might result (Bentler, 1972).

Social desirability. In item construction, no particular precautions were taken to avoid the possibly invalidating influence of socially desirable responding. With respect to evaluating the possible social-desirability influence, Simmons, Brown, Bush, and Blyth (1978) report *r* values of .15 or less between the RSSE and the Crowne-Marlowe Social Desirability Scale. These values were obtained from unspecified subgroups of the Milwaukee seventh graders.

Presumably, the use of trained interviewers promotes honest answering and might to some extent minimize unreliability of responding as well.

Low self-esteem scores from unreliable responding. Since the distribution of scores is strongly skewed, a "low self-esteem" score would be numerically at or near the middle of the scale range. However, a midrange score could also be expected most frequently from persons responding randomly, as might occur due to inattention, uncooperativeness, or inability to understand. This could be an important source of misinterpretation when comparing groups that differ markedly in ability levels, socioeconomic levels, or emotional stability, for example.

Convergent and Discriminant Validity

Multitrait-multimethod matrices. No multitrait-multimethod analyses are presented to explore the convergent and discriminant validity of this instrument.

Convergent validity coefficients. For an unspecified number of secondary-school pupils who responded to a 7-item version of the Rosenberg Self-Esteem Scale and the RSSE, gamma = .6119.

Apparently no other convergent validity studies and no discriminant validity studies have been published.

Assumed Validity Studies

To evaluate the construct validity of the RSSE, Rosenberg and Simmons (1972) relied basically on looking for relationships that one would predict if the RSSE is a valid self-esteem test and if their theoretical ideas about the correlates of self-esteem are correct.

As predicted, the gamma between the RSSE and "our scale of depression" was significant (.3092 for the total Baltimore sample), as was the gamma between the RSSE and a "score of anxiety" (.3398 for the Baltimore sample). (Suggesting discriminant validity is the contrasting fact that the gamma between the RSSE and the RSE was .6119.)

In the Baltimore study, a relation was found between marks in school and the RSSE; namely, high self-esteem was found in 59% of A students, 33% of D students, and 29% of F students (gamma = .1011). However, no association was found between the RSSE and achievement test scores in the Milwaukee sample.

Among secondary-school club members in the Baltimore sample, the gamma between the RSSE and being elected to office was .1705.

Based on Cooley's (1902) ideas, a six-item query asked about the children's perceptions of the favorability of their mothers', parents', peers', and teachers' views of them. Supporting the authors' expectations, the gammas for the total Baltimore sample were all positive: .1672 and .2118 (mothers/parents); .1777 and .1804 (peers); .2460 and .2156 (teachers).

In later publications, Rosenberg, Simmons, and their colleagues have presented evidence about other relationships involving the RSSE (Simmons, Rosenberg, & Rosenberg, 1973; Simmons, Brown, Bush, & Blyth, 1978; Simmons, Blyth, Van Cleave, & Bush, 1979; Simmons & Blyth, 1987). However, these associations do not involve a priori theoretical assumptions about the relationships of specified variables and the RSSE and hence do not strictly qualify as "assumed validity studies."

I have not found publications from other authors concerning the RSSE and its relationships to other variables, as predicted by theory.

Items from the Rosenberg-Simmons Self-Esteem Scale

1. A kid told me: "There's a lot wrong with me." Do you ever feel like this? (IF YES, ASK): Do you feel like this a lot or a little? "There's a lot wrong with me."
2. Another kid said: "I'm not much good at anything." Do you ever feel like this? (IF YES, ASK): Do you feel like this a lot or a little? "I'm not much good at anything."
3. Everybody has some things about him which are good and

some things about him which are bad. Are more of the things about you good, bad, or are they both about the same?

4. Another kid said, "I am no good." Do you ever feel like this? (IF YES, ASK): Do you feel like this a lot or a little? "I am no good."

5. How happy are you with the kind of person you are? Are you very happy, pretty happy, a little happy, or not at all happy with the kind of person you are?

6. Another kid said, "I think I am no good at all." Do you ever feel like this? (IF YES, ASK): Do you feel like this a lot or a little? "I think I am no good at all."

5

JOSEPH PRE-SCHOOL AND PRIMARY SELF-CONCEPT SCREENING TEST (JPPSST)
(Joseph, 1979)

Rationale and General Description

It is generally conceded that preschool children have some descriptive and evaluative self-conceptions, but measuring them is obviously a thorny problem. Although some descriptive/evaluative language occurs at an early age (Goodenough, 1938), one cannot rely on preschoolers' verbalizations to infer self-conceptions in the way language is used for inferring self-concepts in older children and adults. Accordingly, as a basis for inferring self-conceptions, the JPPSST relies on the child's pointing to chosen pictures that were especially drawn for this test.

This instrument, comprising 15 bipolar items, has been used with children between the ages 3-6 and 9-11 but is primarily intended to get global self-concept estimates for preschoolers. It is based on a theoretical premise that "self concept [is] the way an individual perceives himself, his behaviors, how others view him, and the feelings of personal worth and satisfaction that are attached to these perceptions" (Joseph, 1979, p. 8).

The JPPSST measures this personal judgment based on five general dimensions: "Significance [perceived value to] significant others; Competence—the perception of being able to successfully perform; . . . Power—the perceived ability to influence, manipulate, and control others; General Evaluative Content—feelings of satisfaction with one's present life circumstances; and Virtue—perceived adherence to moral standards" (Joseph, 1979, p. 8).

The distribution of items over dimensions is unequal, and no statistical information is presented warranting subscale scores. Relatively little information on this test is available even though nine years have passed since its publication. Nevertheless, it is reviewed here because researchers may wish to use it as a departure point, inasmuch as no more completely developed preschool self-concept tests are extant.

Item/Scale Selection and Refinement

"[The] original items . . . were primarily selected on a rational face validity basis in order to tap the theoretical self-concept dimensions [mentioned above]" (Joseph, 1979, p. 10). Also considered were the items' understandability to young children, their ability to be portrayed by pictures, and their reference to situations thought to be within the range of experience of most children. Items were based in part on a preliminary study of the drawings and accompanying verbalizations of 112 first- and second-grade children who were asked to draw various situations. If children had difficulty differentiating ideas pictorially or verbally, items were combined or eliminated, yielding 15 items. (Items and pictures appear in Joseph, 1979.) An item analysis based on 43 preschool and kindergarten children resulted in "streamlining and simplification" of two questions.

Point-biserial item-total correlations (ranging in various unspecified samples from the .30s to the .70s) were also used as a basis for maintaining or modifying items.

Samples

The norms for the JPPSST were based on the responses of 1,245 urban and rural Illinois children, 91% from white and 9% from various nonwhite groups, and diversified socioeconomically.

Three age groups (3-6 to 4-6, $N = 285$; 4-7 to 5-11, $N = 328$; 6-0 to 9-11, $N = 632$) constituted the normative subgroups. No data about gender frequencies are given, but gender differences are reported to be insignificant. Since the unique potential value of this test is for preschoolers, a larger N in the youngest group would be desirable. Although the author feels his sample "generally reflect[s] the demographic makeup of the United States as a whole" (Joseph, 1979, p. 12), one must reserve judgment about the generalizability of the data.

Descriptive Statistics

For each of five groups, the manual gives ranges of scores that define each of the following designated self-concept levels and also gives percentages of respondents within each level: High Positive (18%), Positive (53%), Watch List (8%), Poor (9%), and High Risk Negative (12%). The procedures for establishing these norms is not clear, and they are based partly on "countless subjective experiences of the author" (Joseph, 1979, p. 20).

Apparently, 76% of all subjects scored 22–30 on a 30-point scale (2 points for each of 15 picture choices). This shows that the distribution of scores is markedly skewed.

Reliability

Internal Consistency
Kuder-Richardson (20) coefficients ranged from .59 to .81 (median = .73), the characteristics of the samples being unspecified.

Test-Retest
For a sample of 18 preschoolers (median age 4-10), $r = .87$ between tests given 4 weeks apart.

Construct Validity

Irrelevant Response/Score Determiners
The following, with their attendant threats to validity, were avoided: forced-choice format, ipsative scoring, item overlap, and use of two-part indices (discrepancy scores). The use of dichotomous scoring may lead to misleading results, as explained by Block (1965).

Acquiescent response set. About half the items begin with the positively scored option, half with the negatively scored one.

Social desirability. No clear method of attempting to control for social-desirability response sets is described.

High uniformity in item endorsement. No systematic information is given about percentages of positive/negative choices, especially with respect to each of the three age groups. Apparently most of the values mentioned are for the total standardization group. All the items yield large percentages of positive choices, at least two thirds of them in the .80s and .90s. This suggests a limitation on coefficients that might be relevant to evaluating convergent and discriminant validity.

Low self-evaluation scores from unreliable responding. It seems highly likely that "low self-evaluation" scores may often result from unreliability of responding rather than from low self-evaluation. Suggesting this is the fact that, among those percentages of positive endorsement that are given separately for youngest and oldest groups, the latter are always higher, for example, 60% and 70%, 84% and 94%, 88% and 98%, 89% and 97%. Although this could represent an age trend toward higher self-evaluation, it seems more plausible that the younger children more often failed to give the majority (positive) response because they were responding unreliably.

Convergent and Discriminant Validity

No multitrait-multimethod analyses or factor analyses are available.

Total JPPSST scores were correlated with each of two scales on which teachers indicated their inferences about the children's self-concepts. One teacher score was based on 30 five-point scales (not further described). For 25 preschoolers (median age 4-10), $r = .51$. The second teacher score came from a 10-item adaptation of Coopersmith's Behavior Rating Form. For the same 25 preschoolers, $r = .65$; for 57 preschoolers and kindergartners (median age 5-4), $r = .31$; and for 68 second and third graders (median age 8-4), $r = .28$. By contrast, with subjects from an affluent, upper-middle-class suburb, a median r of $-.03$ was obtained. Respondents were 44 preschoolers (median age 4-6) and 125 kindergartners (median age 5-5). This lack of correlation may well stem from the fact that self-concept scores tended to be uniformly high in the latter samples, necessarily limiting the size of r.

No information on discriminant validity is presented.

Assumed Validity Studies

Supporting the author's predictions, significant rs were obtained between JPPSST total scores and the following tests of ability: Slosson Intelligence Test IQs, $r = .66$; Preschool Language Scale IQs, $r = .63$; Developmental Test of Visual-Motor Integration, $r = .69$. ($N = 27$ preschoolers, median age 4-11.) However, the fact that they are as large as or larger than the convergent validity coefficients mentioned above raises a question about the discriminant validity of the JPPSST.

Also, though these findings may represent the predicted association between ability and self-esteem, they could alternatively result from the unreliable responding of the less able children, as explained under Irrelevant Response Determiners above.

The same alternative explanation could account for reported significant differences in self-esteem scores between children whose achievement levels were classed by their teachers as within the top 15% or bottom 15%. Likewise, a reported significant difference in JPPSST scores between regular preschool students and those who were developmentally delayed or emotionally disturbed could come from the unreliability of responding of the latter group rather than from their reliably lower self-esteem.

(Readers may wish to read reviews of this test by Gerken and by Telzrow in Mitchell, 1985.)

6

PICTORIAL SCALE OF PERCEIVED COMPETENCE AND SOCIAL ACCEPTANCE FOR YOUNG CHILDREN (PSCA)
(Harter & Pike, 1981, 1983, 1984)

Rationale and General Description

Although some self-descriptive/evaluative language occurs at an early age (Goodenough, 1938), one cannot rely on preschoolers' verbalizations as a basis for inferring their self-concepts in the same way language responses are used to infer self-concepts of older children and adults. Accordingly, Harter and Pike (1984) use a pair of pictures for each of the 24 items of this instrument (e.g., one child is bouncing a ball and one is dropping a ball), and they score the children's choice of responses rather than asking them to express themselves in self-descriptive language. The pictorial format also engages interest and attention and makes it possible to depict skills and specific activities concretely, as is appropriate for very young children.

This instrument involves two versions, one for preschoolers and kindergartners and one for first and second graders. Each taps four a priori dimensions: cognitive competence, physical competence, peer acceptance, and maternal acceptance, with some item overlap between age versions but none between sub-scales within an age version. Two scores are recommended—one for competence and one for acceptance, based on two-factor solutions obtained for each of two item-intercorrelation matrices.

Although Harter thinks the dimensions represented are important in their own right and with respect to their eventual role in children's overall self-esteem, she does not include a global self-worth scale because she believes that "children would not be able to make meaningful judgments about their worth as a person until approximately the age of 8. The very concept of personness is not firmly established among young children" (Harter, 1985b, pp. 144–145). Furthermore, she does not consider a total score from this scale to be a global self-worth score (Harter & Pike, 1984).

Although this scale is in the early stages of validation and use, it is included here because tests for young children are rare and it is the only such test that involves factorially discriminable subscales.

Item/Scale Selection and Refinement

Items for the maternal acceptance scale were generated from a list of behaviors most commonly mentioned by children in response to the request, "Tell me the things your mother does to let you know she likes or loves you" (Harter & Pike, 1984). Aside from this point, Harter and Pike (1984) publish information about the final scales only, saying, "This particular instrument has undergone numerous revisions in terms of scale structure, item content, and question format, based on extensive piloting with large numbers" (p. 1971).

The two versions contain somewhat different items (12 out of 24 are in both versions), because "the specific skills that define or connote competence and social acceptance change rather dramatically within a 4-year range" (Harter & Pike, 1984, p. 1970).

There are four choices per pair of pictures, with the child first being asked to say which child he or she is like, then how much like that child he or she is. Items and pictures appear in Harter and Pike (1981, 1983), which are available from Harter at the University of Denver, Colorado.

Samples

The final standardization group comprised 90 preschoolers (mean age 4.45), 56 kindergartners (mean age 5.54), 65 first graders (mean age 6.32), and 44 second graders (mean age 7.41), approximately equally divided by gender within each group.

With an additional group of 77 preschoolers, 28 kindergartners, and 38 first and second graders, scores for both self-
report and teacher ratings were used.

All subjects were from middle-class neighborhoods, and
96% were white.

This is a small and homogeneous group, so the generalizability of the data obtained remains to be demonstrated.

Descriptive Statistics

Means and standard deviations are given for each of four groups
on each of the four subscales, but not for the combined competence scores and combined acceptance scores, even though factor
analysis suggested the appropriateness of scoring on only two dimensions—perceived competence and perceived acceptance—
and only these two scores are recommended in the manual.

For each of two groups (preschool/kindergarten and grades
1/2), means are given for each item (Harter & Pike, 1984).

For the 16 subscale means (four age groups, four subscales), values range from 2.8 to 3.6, with 11 means exceeding
3.0. Standard deviation values run between .31 and .56. This
shows that the distributions are quite negatively skewed, an important fact when it comes to evaluating the possible influences
of social-desirability response set; possible unreliability of responding as a determinant of "low self-evaluation" scores; and
correlation coefficients involving these scores.

Harter and Pike's (1983) manual recommends looking at
individual profiles across the four subscales, even though they
reached a two-factor solution and no information is given about
how large an individual's interscale difference must be in order to
be reliable, hence potentially interpretable when validity information for each scale is at hand.

Reliability

Internal Consistency
The four Cronbach alphas for competence scores range from .66
to .80, and the four alphas for acceptance range from .84 to .89.

Test-Retest

I have located no test-retest correlations and no information whether mean scores go up on retest. The latter fact has important implications for evaluating individual and group changes over time or as a function of intervention.

Construct Validity

Factor-Analytic Checks on Dimensionality

Although the a priori intentions were to create a four-subscale test, technical criteria and judgments about interpretability favored an oblique two-factor solution in each of two matrices, one based on 145 preschool and kindergarten children, the other based on 104 first and second graders (Harter & Pike, 1984).

The scale intercorrelations for each of the four age groups are substantial, as indicated by the following mean rs (each based on four groups' rs): peer acceptance versus maternal acceptance, .68; cognitive competence versus physical competence, .49; cognitive competence versus peer acceptance, .48; cognitive competence versus maternal acceptance, .40; physical competence versus peer acceptance, .37; physical competence versus maternal acceptance, .35.

In each of the two factor analyses, the two competence scales (cognitive and physical) defined Factor I, and the two acceptance scales (peer and maternal) defined Factor II. With 2 exceptions out of 24, both in the matrix for younger children, each item loaded on only one factor. Item loadings on the designated factor ranged from .19 to .70 in the first matrix and from .22 to .72 in the second.

These results support the idea that this instrument measures two discriminable factors, although the Ns are too small for the number of variables being factored, so confirmatory analyses with larger Ns are needed.

Parenthetically, the following facts support Harter and Pike's (1984) and Shavelson, Hubner, and Stanton's (1976) contention that the structure of the self-concept becomes more differentiated with age. (1) Two, rather than four, correlated factors were obtained from PSCA data (both younger groups considered), whereas five correlated factors from five subscales were obtained from SPPC data (groups from grades 3–8 considered). (2) Scale intercorrelations on the PSCA (both younger groups considered) range from .00 to .80 (mean $r = .46$), whereas scale intercorrelations for the SPPC (groups from grades 3 through 8 considered) range from .14 to .45 (mean $r = .34$). Of course these comparisons are only suggestive, because different items are used in the two scales and one cannot say whether the difference between mean correlation values is significant. (The SPPC is reviewed in this book.)

Irrelevant Response/Score Determiners
The following, with their attendant threats to validity, were avoided: forced-choice format, ipsative scoring, two-part indices (discrepancy scores), use of all items keyed in one direction (positive or negative), and items having double negatives or ambiguous wording.

Social desirability. Harter and Pike (1984) feel that the item format reduces children's tendency to give the socially desirable response. (For their reasoning, see the review of the SPPC in this book.) There is no way to evaluate whether the highly self-favorable responding revealed by the means may represent a deliberate distortion or the children's actually highly favorable self-concepts.

About the meaning of the strong self-favorability bias, Harter (1985a, p. 77) says, "Our interpretation is that [young children] are not yet able to differentiate between the wish to be all competent and their actual ability with regard to these skills. That is, they are unable to distinguish their real from their ideal self."

Low self-evaluation scores from unreliable responding. Since means are so high, at least some of the "low self-evaluation" scores (2.5 on the 4-point scale) might actually come about through unreliable responding rather than representing low self-evaluation. With the data at hand, there is no way to evaluate that threat to validity.

Convergent and Discriminant Validity
Multitrait-multimethod matrices. No multitrait-multimethod matrices are presented.
Convergent validity coefficients. No convergent validity coefficients are presented, partly because there are few published alternate tests of preschool children's self-conceptions. Joseph (1979) includes "significance" (to others) and competence among the items of his preschool scale reviewed in this book, but he does not recommend separate scores for these areas; therefore his test could not have been used to explore the convergent validity of the PSCA subscales. The RSSE (Rosenberg & Simmons, 1972) has also been shown to be appropriate for grades 1 and 2, but it is a unidimensional scale of self-esteem, not purporting to measure what the PSCA does.

Although technical cautions are in order regarding the use of teachers' ratings of children's self-conceptions, these could provide some ideas about convergent and discriminant validity. (See the review of the SDQ in this book.) Correlations between teacher ratings of the children's actual characteristics are not, strictly speaking, convergent validity coefficients, but rather exemplify studies based on assumed validity, discussed in the following section.

Assumed Validity Studies
Perceived cognitive competence. Harter and Pike (1984) assume that if children can cite the reasons for their self-ratings, this supports the assumption that the self-ratings are valid. They cite unpublished data from inquiries made of 43 first graders and 48 second graders, 96% of whom "readily gave specific reasons for why they felt they were [cognitively] competent or not competent" (p. 1977), but no comparable percentage value is given for children giving reasons for their physical competence self-reports. No information is given about reasons for the two acceptance categories for this older group.

No information is given about the percentages of preschool children giving reasons for self-ratings on the two competence scales or the two acceptance scales.

The following predictions were supported concerning associations between perceived cognitive competence and another variable.

The mean cognitive competence score of 12 first graders who were not promoted was significantly lower than that of 12 promoted children of the same age and gender.

There was a significant difference between the mean perceived cognitive competence scores of children rated by teachers as in the top and bottom quartiles of cognitive competence.

In an unspecified number of first and second graders, a correlation of .42 was obtained between perceived cognitive competence and preferred level of difficulty in puzzle tasks (Bierer, 1981, as cited in Harter & Pike, 1984).

Perceived cognitive and physical competencies. As predicted, teacher ratings of children's actual cognitive and physical competencies correlated .37 with children's perceived cognitive competence and .30 with children's perceived physical competence. By contrast, for teacher cognitive competence ratings versus pupil self-perceived physical competence, $r = .11$, and for teacher physical competence ratings versus children's self-perceived cognitive competence ratings, $r = .16$. It is not reported whether the same-domain coefficients significantly exceed the cross-domain ones. If they do, this suggests some discriminant validity between the two competencies that define Factor I.

Gullo and Ambrose (1987) report no correlation between child and teacher ratings for either the cognitive or the physical competence scales of the PSCA. ($N = 30$ children, about 6 years old.)

Peer acceptance. In support of the validity of the peer acceptance scale, 10 children who were "new" to their school (having been there less than 2 months) had a significantly less favorable peer acceptance score than "a comparison group" matched for age and gender who had been in the school at least a year. All subjects were from kindergarten, first grade, or second grade (Harter & Pike, 1984).

Maternal acceptance scale. Supportive of their predictions about the maternal acceptance scale, Harter and Pike (1984) report a correlation of .48 between "our depression/cheerfulness measure" and children's perceived maternal acceptance. (*N* is not specified; children are from kindergarten and grades 1 and 2.)

Thus far, interesting findings have been presented relevant to the construct validity of each of the four subscales. None of these studies has involved the youngest (preschool) group, however.

Although the factor-analytic data point to two discriminable dimensions, no validity information is presented about these dimensions. Instead, all the validity studies refer to one or more of the four original a priori scales.

Since this test is still in the early stages of development, systematic evaluation of convergent and discriminant validity for all subjects and all factor scales is yet to come.

7

SELF-DESCRIPTION
QUESTIONNAIRE (SDQ)

(Marsh, Smith, & Barnes,
1983; Marsh, in press a)

Rationale and General Description

The Self-Description Questionnaire (SDQ)[1] is an eight-scale instrument intended to measure seven aspects of the self-concepts of preadolescent children (ages 7–13) as well as their general sense of self-worth.

The SDQ was developed to test Shavelson, Hubner, and Stanton's (1976) view, according to which "the organization of self-concept is multi-faceted and hierarchical, with perceptions moving from inferences about self in subareas (e.g., academics—reading and mathematics) to broader areas (e.g., academic and nonacademic), and finally to general self-concept" (Marsh, Smith, & Barnes, 1983, p. 334).

The original seven self-concept variables chosen for the SDQ are Physical Abilities/Sports, Physical Appearance, Peer Relations, Parent Relations (four aspects of the nonacademic self-concept), and Reading, Mathematics, and General (All School Subjects) (three aspects of academic self-concept). "An Emotional self-concept [scale], though hypothesized by Shavelson, was excluded since preliminary investigations suggested that young children had difficulty with these items and a satisfactory scale could not be constructed" (Marsh, in press a). Recently, a

---

1. In his forthcoming manuals and future publications concerning the SDQ, SDQ II, and SDQ III, Marsh will use the label SDQ I instead of SDQ. However, the label SDQ is used here since all the research I review uses that label.

General Self scale (a modification of the Rosenberg Self-Esteem Scale) has been added to the SDQ, but data on this scale are available for many fewer subjects than is the case with the seven original scales, and these are mostly restricted to grade 5 (Marsh, in press a).

Consistent with the model of Shavelson, Hubner, and Stanton (1976), it was expected that the separate factors represented by the seven respective scales should be oblique rather than orthogonal and that higher correlations would obtain among the academic factors than among the nonacademic ones.

Item/Scale Selection and Refinement

The first version, containing 100 items, was reduced to 66 items on the basis of an unreported factor analysis, then reduced to 62 items (including only 7 negatively worded ones). This version was used in initial studies (Marsh, Smith, & Barnes, 1983, Sample A). The four nonacademic scales had 8 items apiece, and the three academic scales had 10 items apiece. In each academic scale, 5 items refer to interest and enjoyment ("affective items") and 5 to ability/achievement. Sometimes nonacademic, academic, and grand total scores are also used.

A few minor revisions yielded a 66-item final version, shown in Marsh, Parker, and Smith (1983). This version was used in some of the later studies. Each of the four nonacademic scales has 9 items (including 8 positive), while each of the academic scales has 10 items each (including 8 positive). The first large-scale use of the 8-item General Self scale is reported in Marsh, Smith, and Barnes (1985, Sample E).

Each item is responded to on a 5-point scale from false to true.

Marsh (1986c), using Sample G, looked separately at the so-called negative items, that is, statements to which one must respond "false" or "mostly false" in order to make a self-favorable assertion. When negative items were excluded, the alpha coefficients for every scale and the average interitem correlation for every scale were higher, with the greatest improvement in alpha coefficients occurring for the youngest children. The total positive-item and total negative-item scores correlated only .27 for the total sample. For the grade 2 children, $r = -.02$, and for the grade 5 children, $r = .60$, again showing that the effect is age related. In one confirmatory factor analysis of a new sample of fifth graders (Sample E), a "negative item factor" substantially correlated with reading achievement. Consideration of all the findings above led to the decision to exclude negative items from SDQ scores, albeit not from the test form itself.[2] The implications of this are considered further under the heading Irrelevant Response/Score Determiners below.

On the basis of factor analyses done to confirm the correctness of assignment of items to scales, factor scores for each item were computed, and these were used in much of the research of Marsh and his colleagues. Marsh (in press a) states, "While factor scores and the unweighted scale scores are substantially correlated, factor analytically derived scores distinguish better among SDQ facets than do the unweighted scale scores, and they are more clearly related to various criterion measures" (p. 14). On the other hand, after looking at age and sex effects with both unweighted scores and factor scores, Marsh (1985) reported that "results based upon the two sets of scores are so similar that the distinction is not important in the discussion of the findings" (p. 199). Future researchers may want to see whether the type of score makes a difference with respect to the relation between SDQ scores and other variables they are trying to relate to these scores. In any event, factor scores can be produced by a computer-scoring program mentioned in Marsh's (in press a) manual, should a user want to employ them.

2. Marsh (1986c) lists and comments on the 12 negative SDQ items as follows: "(1) I hate mathematics; (2) My parents are usually unhappy or disappointed with what I do; (3) I hate sports and games; (4) Most kids have more friends than I do; (5) I hate all school subjects; (6) I am ugly; (7) I am dumb at reading; (8) Overall I am no good; (9) I am dumb in all school subjects; (10) I can't do anything right; (11) I hate reading; and (12) I am dumb at mathematics. . . . Item 10, perhaps Item 8, and maybe Item 2 seem to be negatively worded negative items, but the rest appear to be affirmatively worded negative items" (p. 38).

Samples

In a series of articles, Marsh and his colleagues have reported on 3,562 different subjects from Sydney, Australia, and environs, 303 English urban subjects, and 471 Canadian subjects from Ottawa. The subjects may be divided into sample groups as follows, each group having been used in one or more studies. To save repetition later on, I describe each sample immediately below, labeling each by a letter or name for ready reference.

Sample A
$N = 655$ pupils from coeducational inner-city public schools, 47% female, all fifth and sixth graders, mean age 11 years, lower and lower-middle class (Marsh, Smith, & Barnes, 1983; Marsh, Parker, & Smith, 1983; Marsh, Relich, & Smith, 1983). A subset of Sample A was used by Marsh, Smith, Barnes, and Butler (1983). This subset ($N = 528$) is here labeled *Sample A'*.

Sample B
$N = 305$ pupils in coeducational schools, divided into two subsamples: B-1, $N = 180$, 48% female, sixth graders, 10–13 years (mean = 11.7), low socioeconomic section of suburb. B-2, $N = 125$, 49% female, sixth graders, 10–13 years (mean = 11.6), higher socioeconomic section of same suburb (Marsh, 1984b; Marsh & Parker, 1984; Marsh, Parker, & Smith, 1983).

Sample C
$N = 498$ pupils, 45% female, from 11 private Catholic schools providing a good cross section of the Sydney school district in terms of social class and academic achievement, all sixth graders, 10–13 years old (mean = 11.6), 90% attending single-sex classes (Marsh, Relich, & Smith, 1983).

Sample D
$N = 248$ pupils, percentage of females unspecified, fifth graders, mostly 10 years old, attending public coeducational schools, low to upper-middle class (Marsh, 1986d; Marsh, Cairns, Relich, Barnes, & Debus, 1984).

Sample E
N = 559 pupils, 25% female, fifth graders in private Catholic schools, lower-middle to upper-middle class, 95% attending single-sex classes (Marsh, 1984a, 1986c, 1986d; Marsh, Smith, & Barnes, 1984, 1985).

Sample F
N = 143 pupils, percentage of females unspecified, attending Catholic coeducational schools, 8–11 years old, predominantly middle class (Marsh, Smith, Barnes, & Butler, 1983).

Sample G
N = 658 pupils, percentage of females unspecified: 170 second graders, 103 third graders, 143 fourth graders, 251 fifth graders; ages respectively approximately 7, 8, 9, 10 years; all from public coeducational schools in Sydney, Australia; lower to upper-middle class (Marsh, 1986c; Marsh, Barnes, Cairns, & Tidman, 1984; Marsh & Hocevar, 1985; Marsh & Shavelson, 1985).

Sample H
N = 303 urban English pupils from 11 different classes of the final year of primary school, modal age 10 years, and 303 urban Australian respondents of comparable grade and age; each sample comprised 171 males and 132 females; socioeconomic data not given (Marsh, in press a; Marsh & Smith, 1987).

Sample I
N = 510 pupils, 42% female, grades 7, 8, 9 from single-sex high schools, middle class (Marsh & Gouvernet, in press).

Sample CAN
N = 471 gifted and normal Canadian children (241 grade 5, 130 grade 8), socioeconomic class and percentage of females unspecified (Byrne & Schneider, 1988).

Sample OBB
N = 66 high-school males, aged 13–16 years, mostly ninth graders, participating in one of five Outward Bound Bridging

courses (only 43 were used in the data analyses below) (Marsh and Richards, in press b).

Normative Archive SDQ *Sample*
N = 3,562 of the 3,576 Australian respondents who make up Samples A through I inclusive (Marsh, 1985; Marsh & Gouvernet, in press; Marsh, in press a).

A randomly drawn subsample of this archive, comprising 500 females and 500 males, all fifth graders, was used by Marsh (1987b).

Obviously, although the total number of subjects is large, including both males and females and a wide range of socioeconomic and ability levels, it is restricted with respect to geographical location, urbanness, and ethnicity. Accordingly, the generalizability of the reported findings, although quite plausible, remains to be demonstrated.

Descriptive Statistics

Means, medians, standard deviations, and evaluations of degree of skew of the distribution are not given for most of the samples A through I or Sample CAN, either for the seven scales, for the total nonacademic and academic subscales, for total SDQ scores, or for the self-esteem scale (General Self scale) included in the report by Marsh, Smith, and Barnes (1985).

Means (but no other descriptive statistics) are given separately for boys and girls of Sample A and Sample C (Marsh, Relich, & Smith, 1983), but these are based on standard scores (mean = 50, SD = 10) rather than on raw scores or the factor scores usually used by Marsh and his colleagues.

In the forthcoming SDQ manual (Marsh, in press a), means, medians, standard deviations, and indices of skew are given for the raw scores of the Normative Archive SDQ Sample (i.e., Samples A through I inclusive) and for sex and grade-level subsamples of the Normative Archive SDQ Sample.

Actually, most of their work with these scales was done with factor scores based on their factor analyses of items or item pairs. Other users will need to get this weighting information from the authors or perhaps establish their own way of determining factor scores based on factor analyses of their own data sets.

Reliability

Internal Consistency
In general, alpha coefficients are very high. The mean alpha values across five samples (A, B-1, B-2, F at first test, F at retest) are as follows: Physical Abilities/Sports, .82; Physical Appearance, .91; Peer Relations, .85; Parent Relations, .84; Reading, .91; Mathematics, .93; General School (All School Subjects), .86.

Using only positive items, Marsh, Barnes, Cairns, and Tidman (1984) obtained the following alpha coefficients for Sample G: Physical Abilities/Sports, .77; Physical Appearance, .87; Peer Relations, .82; Parent Relations, 76; Total Nonacademic self-concept, .90; Reading, .86; Mathematics, .89; All School Subjects, .84; Total Academic self-concept, .92; Total self-concept, .93. For a subset of negative items excluded from the calculations above, alpha coefficient = .73.

For the Normative Archive SDQ Sample (N = 3,562), alphas were Physical Abilities/Sports, .83; Physical Appearance, .90; Peer Relations, .85; Parent Relations, .80; Reading, .89; Mathematics, .89; General School (All School Subjects), .86; General Self, .81 (N = 729 only for the General Self); Total Nonacademic, .91; Total Academic, .92; Total Self, .94.

Also, for the Normative Archive SDQ Sample, "Each individual item is significantly correlated with the other items designed to measure the same facets of self-concept" (Marsh, in press a, p. 35).

Test-Retest
Marsh, Smith, Barnes, and Butler (1983) tested Samples A' and F 6 months apart within the same year, obtaining the following test-retest coefficients: Physical Abilities/Sports, .74, .51; Physical Appearance, .61, .60; Peer Relations, .61, .62; Parent Relations, .55, .27; Reading, .61, .69; Mathematics, .68, .61; General School, .54, .71.

Marsh and Richards (in press b, Sample OBB) report the following 6-week test-retest coefficients for 48 respondents: All School Subjects, .69; Reading, .76; Mathematics, .85; Physical Abilities/Sports, .73; Appearance, .68; Peer Relations, .45; Parent Relations, .69.

Regarding the stability of *mean values* over time, Marsh, Smith, Barnes, and Butler (1983) say only that "absolute stability implies that the average of self-concept across all students does not vary over the interval considered. There is good support for this type of stability in that differences were small and unsystematic for each of the seven areas of self-concept in both studies" (p. 785).

Construct Validity

Factor-Analytic Checks on Dimensionality
Numerous exploratory and confirmatory analyses of SDQ data have been reported, some performed to explore and support the predicted dimensionality of the instrument, some to check other points, such as the characteristics of negative items; the invariance of dimensionality across groups differing in age, sex, or national origin; or possible higher-order factor structures.

The analyses did not all involve the same version of the SDQ, and some used item scores while others used item-pair scores as the input.[3]

The earliest analyses (on Samples A, A', B, C, F at Time 1, and F at Time 2) were based on item scores from both negative and positive items, representing the original seven dimensions

---

3. Marsh (1986c) gives the advantages and disadvantages of the use of item pairs, as follows: "The use of responses to item pairs . . . is preferable to the factor analysis of responses to individual items because (a) the ratio of the number of subjects to variables is increased; (b) each of the variables used in the factor analysis is more reliable; (c) factor loadings will be less affected by idiosyncratic or unique variance in responses to individual items; and (d) the cost of factor analysis, particularly CFAs [confirmatory factor analyses], will be substantially reduced. The major disadvantages in the use of item pairs are that information about individual items is lost and that it is assumed that items within each scale are homogeneous with respect to the dimension that they are designed to measure" (pp. 42–43).

(i.e., excluding the "self-esteem" scale called the General Self scale).

By contrast, the analyses of data from Samples H, I, the randomly drawn sample of 1,000 fifth graders from the Normative Archive SDQ Sample, and one of the analyses of Sample E were based on pairs of positive items and also included item pairs of the General Self scale. Negative items were excluded on the basis of evidence cited above under Item/Scale Selection and Refinement.

In the analyses of data from the samples mentioned above, all items (or item pairs) of each of the seven (or eight) SDQ scales loaded highly or fairly highly on a target factor and showed negligible loadings on the other six (or seven) factors. This series of findings clearly supports the intended multidimensionality of the SDQ.

In the factor analyses of Samples A and C, an eighth factor emerged, defined by the interest-enjoyment items of each of the academic self-concept scales (Reading, Mathematics, All School Subjects).

In Sample E (Marsh, Smith, & Barnes, 1985) and in Sample I (Marsh & Gouvernet, in press), an eighth factor was defined by the modified Rosenberg Self-Esteem Scale (General Self scale of the SDQ). In each study, a matrix of factor pattern correlations shows the following: (1) The self-esteem factor correlates with each of the seven SDQ factors, each correlation exceeding the median r in the rest of the matrix. This tends to support the hierarchical model. (2) The self-esteem factor correlates most strongly with Physical Abilities/Sports, Physical Appearance, Peer Relations, and All School Subjects factors. (Although Total Nonacademic, Total Academic, and overall Total scores from the seven more specific scales are available, correlations between these and the General Self scale are not presented.)

It would be interesting to determine the value of a multiple correlation in which the seven more specific SDQ scores are used to predict the General Self score.

To evaluate the prediction that academic self-concept dimensions might be separate from the nonacademic ones, higher-order factor analyses were done on Sample A' at test and retest and on Sample F at test and retest (Marsh, Smith, Barnes, & Butler, 1983). Factor I was defined by self-concept scales concerning Physical Abilities, Appearance, and Peer Relations. Factor II was defined by the Reading and All School Subjects scales. Factor III was defined by the Mathematics and All School Subjects scales. Factor IV was defined (in three samples) by the Parent Relations scale. These groupings appear to make sense intuitively.

The generalizability of the factor structures across age, sex, and nationality have also been explored. (Marsh & Smith [1987] make the point that "unless the factor structures are similar, there may be no basis for comparing mean differences" [p. 62].)

Using only the positive items and the original seven scales from Sample G, Marsh, Barnes, Cairns, and Tidman (1984) made a separate factor analysis of item-pair scores for each of four grades, 2–5. As in previous analyses, factor loadings for each variable were relatively high on the respective target factors and low on nontarget factors, and correlations among factors were congruent with the Shavelson model. However, the factors were more clearly defined in the results for grades 4 and 5.

By means of confirmatory factor analysis of the same data from Sample G, Marsh and Hocevar (1985) tested a variety of higher-order factor models to explore the possibility of factorial invariance across the four grade levels. They conclude that "as was anticipated from the findings of first-order models, the higher-order tests of invariance do not support the hypothesis that the four grade levels have the same higher order structure" (p. 576).[4]

Using only the eight positively worded items from each of the original seven SDQ scales, Marsh (1987b) applied various models of confirmatory factor analysis to the paired-item scores of 1,000 fifth graders drawn randomly from the Normative Archive SDQ Sample. The sample was divided into four groups as

---

4. In this article, Marsh and Hocevar (1985) also give a detailed discussion of confirmatory factor analysis (as opposed to exploratory factor analysis), its advantages for specified purposes, possibly useful modifications of it, and the subjectivity involved in deciding upon goodness of fit.

bases for four factor analyses: 250 males and 250 females in one group and 250 males and 250 females in a replication group.

He concludes that "an a priori factor structure . . . was invariant across responses by random split halves of the same group, and . . . the a priori structure was reasonably invariant across responses by males and females" (p. 476).

To explore cross-national generalizability, Marsh and Smith (1987) used two sets of confirmatory factor analyses of SDQ item-pair scores based only on positive items and including the General Self scale items. From the results obtained with Sample H (English and Australian preadolescents), they conclude that "in the first set of analyses, the factor structure for the two groups was found to be reasonably invariant. In the second set of analyses, Australian and English students were shown to have similar self-concepts for 7 of the 8 SDQ factors [Australians had higher General School scores], and sex differences on SDQ factors were found to be similar for English and Australian preadolescents" (p. 73).

Irrelevant Response/Score Determiners
The following, with their attendant threats to validity, were avoided: forced-choice format, dichotomous scoring, item overlap between scales (except between subscale scores and total scores), item ambiguity, ipsative scoring, and two-part indices (discrepancy scores), except for one study (Marsh, Smith, Barnes, & Butler, 1983).

No attempt was made to control acquiescent response set or social-desirability bias. In the earlier and intermediate seven-scale versions of SDQ, 56 out of 66 items are positive, and when the General Self scale is included, 64 out of 74 items are positive. On the basis of methodological studies of negative items (cited above under Item/Scale Selection and Refinement), the final version of the SDQ excludes all negative items.

However, Marsh and his colleagues argue that the distinct patterns of correlations obtained ("clean" factor patterns) and the absence of a general factor militate against the idea that important influences of acquiescent response set and social-desirability bias affect their self-concept scores.

No attempt has been made to evaluate (and if necessary to circumvent) the possibility that at least some of the "low self-concept" scores might represent unreliable responding due to lack of understanding, inattention, or uncooperativeness, as opposed to validly representing a poor self-evaluation. This problem needs to be considered, since for each scale the distribution is very skewed (means of the scales that range from 8 to 40 vary from 27.49 to 32.99 for the Normative Archive SDQ Sample, according to Marsh, in press a, Appendix I).

On a scale of 8 to 40, scores of 23 and 24 would be the most likely ones to be obtained from purely random responding, but on any given scale these scores would be interpreted by Marsh and his colleagues as low self-concept scores because they represent percentile values ranging from 4th (Parent Relations) to 35th (Physical Appearance). This ambiguity is important because the possibility that an appreciable number of lower scores may come from unreliable responding has implications for how one might obtain artifactual correlations between SDQ scale scores and other theoretically related variables such as academic ability, emotional disturbance, or perhaps even socioeconomic class.

Marsh (in press a) has proposed but not yet empirically evaluated the interpretability of a number of "control scores" aimed at identifying subjects who may have responded in one or more "inappropriate ways," such as by random responding or use of a nonrandom response pattern independent of item content.

Convergent and Discriminant Validity
   Convergent validity coefficients.   Marsh and his associates used teacher rating scales of students' self-concepts as the criterion to explore convergent validity in most studies, and they used peer responses about the respondents' self-concepts to infer students' self-concepts in one study (Marsh, Smith, & Barnes, 1984).

Marsh, Smith, and Barnes (1983) argue that ratings by others . . . will only agree with self-reports if the external observer knows the subject well, observes a wide range of behaviors, has observed a wide enough range of subjects to have established a frame of reference, is able to make skillful perceptions and discriminations, and is judging the same characteristics as the subject. To the extent that these criteria are not satisfied, the inferred self-concept will not be a good indicator of self-concept. (p. 337)

Teachers were provided with one rating scale for each of the seven SDQ dimensions and were asked to rate each pupil on a 9-point response scale for each of the dimensions, following the instructions, "Please evaluate the pupil's self-concept, using your perceptions of the student's own feelings in each of the areas listed below" (Marsh & Parker, 1984, p. 219). To reduce differences among teachers with respect to response bias in scale use, teacher ratings were "adjusted" by setting the mean and SD of each teacher's ratings to equal the mean and SD of the factor scores in that schoolroom. Use of such adjusted teacher ratings reduced teachers' interscale correlations and increased agreement between teacher ratings and student self-concept factor scores—that is, it increased convergent validities.

Marsh, Smith, and Barnes (1984) not only used teachers' inferences but also asked peers to fill out the SDQ as they thought specified others would when describing themselves.

Marsh, Smith, and Barnes (1983) recognize possible limitations in these inferred self-concept scores, but they argue that using alternate forms of student self-concept reports as a means for evaluating convergent validity would really amount to obtaining reliability measures. Perhaps for that reason, few correlations are offered between the SDQ scales and other possibly relevant self-report scales: Byrne and Schneider (1988) and Marsh and Gouvernet (in press) correlated scores from four SDQ scales (Physical Abilities, Peer Relations, General, Total Academic) with four apparently corresponding scales from Harter's PCSC (an earlier version of the SPPC reviewed in this book). For the gifted children in Sample CAN, these convergent validity values ranged from .54 to .86 for grade 5 (mean = .73) and from .66 to .88 for grade 6 (mean = .80). For Sample I, these correlations ranged from .57 to .74 (mean = .64), whereas the cross-correlations relevant to discriminant validity ranged from .07 to .48 (mean =

.30). Marsh and Richards (in press b, Sample OBB) found some convergence between the SDQ Parent Relations scale and Coopersmith's SEI Social scale and between the SDQ Peer Relations scale and the SEI Social scale, but there was little evidence for convergent and discriminant validity of the SDQ academic scales and the SEI academic scales.

Convergent validity coefficients involving *teachers' inferences* are reported for each of the seven scales for each of seven nonoverlapping data sets: Samples A, A' at retest, F at test and retest, B-1, B-2, and E.

The mean convergent validity coefficients and their ranges, based on these seven data sets involving teachers' inferences, are Physical Abilities, .41 (.30 to .53); Appearance, .23 (.06 to .31); Peer Relations, .30 (.15 to .47); Parent Relations, .19 (.01 to .27); Reading, .42 (.22 to .58); Mathematics, .40 (.29 to .74); All School Subjects, .36 (.21 to .65).

These appear to be encouraging convergent validity coefficients, especially considering that the teacher data involved only one rating per scale per pupil (reliability indeterminate) and there was considerable intercorrelation among teachers' ratings compared with the much lower intercorrelations among students' ratings.

The convergent validity coefficients involving *peer inferences* concerning respondents' self-concepts are Physical Abilities, .32; Appearance, .17; Peer Relations, .24; Parent Relations, .16; Reading, .28; Mathematics, .34; All School Subjects, .30; General Self, .11 (Marsh, Smith, & Barnes, 1984). As with the teacher-self correlations, those involving Physical Abilities, Reading, Mathematics, and All School Subjects were also the four highest peer-self correlations. In the Marsh, Smith, and Barnes (1984) study, the convergent validity coefficient involving teacher inferences about children's General Self is .19 (compared with the correlation given for peer-inference data, .11).

Multitrait-multimethod matrices. I found seven multitrait-multimethod matrices in which nonoverlapping data sets were used and teachers' inferences about the pupils' self-concepts constituted the validation criterion. The seven data sets are from

Samples A (Marsh, Smith, & Barnes, 1983; repeated in Marsh, Parker, & Smith, 1983); B-1 and B-2 (Marsh, Parker, & Smith, 1983); A', F at test, F at retest (Marsh, Smith, Barnes, & Butler, 1983); and E (Marsh, Smith, & Barnes, 1984).

Sample E data analyses also used peers' inferences about respondents' self-concepts as one validity criterion. These data are considered separately below.

None of the matrices has been subjected to any analysis (e.g., the method of Kavanaugh, MacKinney, & Wolins, 1971) that might evaluate the relative contributions of subject, aspect of self-concept, method (self-responses and others' responses about self), and error. Therefore the discussion below is based only on visually observable trends in the data.

To get a general idea about the discriminant as well as convergent validity of the SDQ, I first took an overview of the seven matrices to see whether the mean correlation coefficients across all scales and all matrices fall in the following order from highest to lowest, as they should if discriminant validity of all scales is to be supported: (1) monotrait-monomethod (alpha reliability), (2) monotrait-heteromethod (convergent validity), (3) heterotrait-monomethod (cross-scale intercorrelations among pupil self-concept scores), and (4) heterotrait-heteromethod (cross-correlations between teachers' ratings of pupils' self-concepts on a given scale and pupils' self-concept scores on other scales).[5]

Averaging across seven scales and seven matrices, I found the mean rs to be as follows: monotrait-monomethod (alpha reliabilities), .87; monotrait-heteromethod (convergent validities), .34; heterotrait-monomethod (self-concept correlations across different scales), .23; heterotrait-heteromethod (teachers vs. pupils, different scales), .12. Thus, the overall picture from combining across seven multitrait-multimethod matrices offers

---

5. However, it has been argued that it is only desirable, not necessary, realistic, or even logical, to require that heterotrait-monomethod correlations should be smaller that convergent validity correlations. (See Humphreys, 1960; Jackson, 1969; Wylie, 1974, p. 110.)

some encouraging visual support for the convergent and discriminant validity of the SDQ scales.[6]

Of course, these encouraging results from this broad overview do not say whether the criteria will be fulfilled for each matrix or for each scale within or across matrices. When one looks separately at each of the seven matrices (averaging across scales within each matrix), one sees that the order of mean *r*s within each of six of the matrices supports convergent and discriminant validity. However, the difference between the mean convergent validity coefficient and the mean heterotrait-monomethod coefficient is often very small. In particular, data from Samples A', F at test, F at retest, and E (where the two values were actually slightly reversed) failed to fulfill the criterion that the mean convergent validity coefficient should exceed the mean heterotrait-monomethod correlation. The convergent and discriminant validity of the various scales appeared to vary markedly.

Overall, the matrices for Samples A, B-1, and B-2 seem to give the strongest visual support to the convergent and discriminant validity of the SDQ scales. Thus the following summary statements about two groups of scales are based on these three matrices, with some additional information from the other four matrices given in parentheses at the ends of the next two paragraphs.

Physical Abilities, Reading, Mathematics, and All School Subjects have the highest convergent validity coefficients (range = .31 to .74, mean = .48): 97% of the heterotrait-monomethod coefficients and 100% of the heterotrait-heteromethod coefficients are equal to or smaller than their respective convergent validities. Not so clearly supporting discriminant validity was the considerable overlap between sizes of heterotrait-monomethod *r*s and corresponding heterotrait-

---

6. I omitted consideration of heterotrait-monomethod correlations among teachers' inferences about the subjects' self-concepts, since I was evaluating the validity of pupils' scores. The teacher correlations between scales exceeded the student correlations between scales, indicating more halo or common method bias among the teacher ratings.

heteromethod rs for each scale. (The remaining four matrices also show 97% of the heterotrait-heteromethod coefficients involving these four scales to be equal to or lower than their respective convergent validity values. These other four matrices offer no support to the discriminant validity of each scale in terms of the heterotrait-monomethod coefficients' being lower than the convergent validity coefficients.)

The patterns shown by the matrices for Samples A, B-1, and B-2 for the variables Physical Appearance, Peer Relations, and Parent Relations resembled one another as follows: The convergent validity coefficients, although significant, were lower than for the other four scales (range = .16 to .47; mean = .29). Only 74% of the heterotrait-monomethod rs were smaller than or equal to their respective convergent validity coefficients, but 94% of the heterotrait-heteromethod rs were smaller than or equal to their respective convergent validity coefficients. Again, there was much overlap between the heterotrait-heteromethod coefficients and the corresponding heterotrait-monomethod rs. (For the remaining four matrices, 3 convergent validity coefficients out of 12 are insignificant—2 for Physical Appearance and 1 for Parent Relations; only 83% of the heterotrait-heteromethod coefficients are equal to or smaller than their respective validity coefficients; and only 60% of the heterotrait-heteromethod rs are equal to or smaller than their respective convergent validity coefficients.)

As already mentioned, the Sample E data include a matrix that used peers' inferences about respondents' self-concepts. For this matrix, the mean alpha coefficient for the self-concept scales is .85. The mean convergent validity value for peer-self correlations across eight scales (including the General Self scale) is .24 (each value being significant), the mean heterotrait-monomethod r (correlations between self scales) is .22, and the mean heterotrait-heteromethod r (correlations of peers vs. self on different scales) is .07. Thus the means of the eight scales fall in the desired order. The peer data resemble the teacher data in that Physical Abilities, Reading, Mathematics, and All School Subjects scales yield higher validity coefficients than the Physical Appearance, Peer Relations, and Parent Relations scales.

As already indicated, no significance tests have been applied within each matrix, and even had such tests been used they could not give the information necessary to identify significant and valid interscale differences in an individual respondent's scores, as in plotting and attempting to interpret a pupil's self-concept profile.

In short, the picture is supportive of the overall convergent and discriminant validity of the SDQ scales, especially Physical Abilities, Reading, Mathematics, and All School Subjects, but it would be premature to base intraindividual inferences on such data.

Assumed Validity Studies
It is interesting that virtually all the studies relating SDQ scores to other variables in order to test theory-based predictions involve only the three academic self-concept scales, Reading, Mathematics, and All School Subjects. Almost everything remains to be done to explore the construct validity of the other four SDQ variables by using them to test theory-based predictions.

Attribution scores. Several studies examine predicted patterns of association between SDQ scores and attribution scores.

For attribution scores from Crandall, Katkovsky, and Crandall's (1965) Intellectual Achievement Responsibility Scale, Marsh, Smith, and Barnes (1983) theorized that self-concept scores should correlate positively with attributions of ability/effort for success, less positively with lack-of-effort attributions for failure, and negatively (or least positively) with lack-of-ability attributions for failure. Two data sets (Sample A and Sample C) offer support for these predictions so far as the scales for Reading, Mathematics, and All School Subjects are concerned. For each data set, the sizes of the coefficients are in the direction predicted (Marsh, Smith, & Barnes, 1983; Marsh, Relich, & Smith, 1983).

Marsh, Cairns, Relich, Barnes, and Debus (1984) (Sample D) developed an alternate measure of attribution, the Sydney Attribution Scale (SAS), which they used to test predictions about internal attributions for success and failure in Mathematics, Reading, and All School Subjects. As expected, self-concept scores for each of the three academic dimensions (1) correlated positively with attributions of ability and effort for success on that dimension, with Mathematics and Reading self-concept scores also correlated substantially with attributions of ability and effort for general academic success; and (2) correlated negatively with attributions of ability and effort for failure on that dimension, with Mathematics and Reading self-concept scores also correlating substantially with attributions of ability and effort for general academic failure. Cross-correlations—for example, attributions concerning reading success versus self-concepts regarding mathematics—were uniformly smaller than within-dimension correlations.

From a factor analysis of a revised version of the Sydney Attribution Scale, Marsh (1984a, Sample E) obtained factors of internal attributions of ability for success, effort for success, ability for failure, effort for failure. Each of these pertained simultaneously to both mathematics and reading. As predicted, and analogous to Marsh, Cairns, Relich, Barnes, and Debus's (1984) results, substantial positive correlations were obtained between (1) Reading, Mathematics, All School Subjects, and Total Academic self-concept SDQ scores and (2) attributions of ability and effort for success, while fairly substantial negative correlations were obtained between (1) Mathematics, Reading, All School Subjects, and Total Academic self-concept SDQ scores and (2) attributions of ability and effort for failure. Almost all correlations between each of the nonacademic SDQ scores and each of the attribution-scale factor scores were smaller than those involving the academic scales of the SDQ.

Marsh and Gouvernet (in press, Sample I) predicted positive correlations between each of the SDQ academic self-concept scales and scores from Ryan's Self-Regulation Questionnaire, which purports to measure a continuum from attributions of external regulation to attributions of intrinsic regulation. Their prediction was sustained, since the correlations involving Reading, Mathematics, and All School Subjects scales were .28, .36, and .48, whereas the correlations with the other five SDQ scales ranged from .11 to .21 (the latter for the General Self scale).

Intellectual variables. It seems reasonable to expect that academic self-concept dimensions should correlate with such intellectual variables as standardized achievement tests in reading and mathematics, with teachers' estimates of students' reading and mathematics abilities, and with IQ. Marsh, Smith, Barnes, and Butler (1983) say, "Self-concept theorists assume that self-concept should be correlated with abilities in areas seen as important to a person, and that self-concept in particular areas should be most highly correlated with abilities in the same areas" (p. 774).

In 11 samples (A, A' at retest, B-1, B-2, D, E, F at test, F at retest, I, OBB at test, and OBB at retest), *standardized reading test scores* were correlated with each self-concept variable. Significant *r*s were obtained for every sample between reading achievement scores and Reading self-concept, and for seven of these samples, between reading achievement scores and All School Subjects self-concept scores. Correlations between reading achievement scores and the other self-concept variables are negligible except that in Samples B-1 and B-2 reading achievement scores correlated significantly with Mathematics self-concept scores and in Sample OBB reading achievement scores correlated significantly with Parent Relations (at test), and with Peer Relations (at retest).

In six nonoverlapping data sets (A' at retest, B-1, B-2, E, F at test, F at retest), *teachers' ratings of pupils' reading abilities* yield a pattern of correlations similar to those just described for the reading and achievement scores.

This pattern of findings across 11 samples (for reading scores) and 6 samples (for teachers' reading ability estimates) supports an argument for the discriminant validity of the Reading self-concept scores and for the idea that they are based to some extent on "objective reality."

In Sample E, *mathematics achievement scores* did not correlate discriminantly with Mathematics self-concept scores. However, in Samples C, I, OBB at test, and OBB at retest, mathematics scores did correlate significantly with Mathematics and All School Subjects self-concept scores.

Teachers' mathematics ability ratings were available for six samples: A, B-1, B-2, E, F at test, F at retest. Almost without exception, these ratings correlated significantly with Mathematics self-concept scores and with All School Subjects self-concept scores, but not with other self-concept dimensions. Four significant correlations with Reading self-concept scores were also obtained.

Thus, the pattern of results from mathematics achievement tests and teachers' ratings of mathematics abilities supports an argument for the discriminant validity of the Mathematics self-concept scores and for the idea that they are based, to some extent, on "objective reality."

Correlations between IQ and self-concept dimensions are available only for Samples B-1 and B-2. Of six correlations involving either the Reading self-concept, Mathematics self-concept, or All School Subjects self-concept, all are significant, and IQ did not correlate with the other four (nonacademic) SDQ variables (Marsh & Parker, 1984).

In another analysis of the data from Samples B-1 and B-2, an *unweighted average of IQ and standardized reading achievement scores* correlated significantly with Total Academic self-concept scores but not with Total Nonacademic self-concept scores within each of the two SES levels (Marsh, 1984b).

Also with the same samples, Marsh (1984b) found that students' average self-ratings of academic ability correlated significantly with academic but not with nonacademic self-concept scores within each of the two SES groups. These findings, of course, involve two self-reports from the same subjects, a less stringent test of validity than the correlations involving IQ, achievement-test scores, and teacher ratings.

The intuitively reasonable pattern from the studies cited above involving ability/achievement measures offers support for the discriminant validity of the academic self-concept scales and for the idea they are based to some extent on "objective reality."

Sports ability. For Sample B (i.e., B-1 plus B-2), scores from a single-item self-rating scale of Sports Ability were uncorrelated with academic self-concept scores but were significantly correlated with Physical Abilities, Peer Relations, and Total Nonacademic self-concept scores. Since Sports Ability is a self-report scale similar in content to some items in the Physical Abilities scale, this pattern of correlations does not offer a stringent test of the construct validity of the Physical Abilities self-concept scores (Marsh, 1984b).

Sex differences. As already reported in the section on Factor-Analytic Checks on Dimensionality, an a priori factor structure was reasonably invariant across responses by males and females in a subsample of 1,000 fifth-grade subjects from the Normative Archive SDQ Sample. Therefore it is appropriate to consider here the mean sex differences on the SDQ scales.

Marsh, Smith, and Barnes (1983) and Marsh, Relich, and Smith (1983) expected to find gender differences on separate SDQ scales according to sexual stereotypes. Specifically, boys were expected to have higher self-concepts in Physical Abilities and Mathematics, girls to have higher self-concepts in Reading.

Four publications give information on predicted and unpredicted sex differences: Marsh, Relich, and Smith (1983), based on Samples A and C; Marsh, Barnes, Cairns, and Tidman (1984), based on Sample G; Marsh, Smith, and Barnes (1985), based on Sample E; and Marsh (1985), based on the Normative Archive SDQ Sample, which includes the samples above as well as many other subjects.

All four of these publications report significant support for the prediction that boys will have higher self-concepts on the Physical Abilities scale and girls will have higher self-concepts on the Reading scale. All four studies also support the prediction that boys will have higher self-concepts on the Mathematics scale, but two of the differences obtained were said to be "small" or insignificant. On the remaining scales, no consistently reported significant sex differences emerge across the four studies.

The strong replicated sex differences in Physical Abilities, Mathematics, and Reading are in line with what sexual stereotypes would lead one to predict.

Age effects. As already reported, confirmatory factor analysis failed to support the hypothesis of factorial invariance across grades 2–5 (Marsh & Hocevar, 1985, Sample G). According to Marsh and Smith (1987) and Marsh (1987b), this lack of factorial invariance raises questions about the interpretability of mean age differences on the SDQ scales.

No theoretical predictions about age effects were offered as a basis for the studies listed below, so they do not, strictly speaking, constitute "assumed validity" research. Moreover, caution is in order in interpreting age effects obtained from cross-sectional designs.

Using data from Sample G (grades 2–5), Marsh, Barnes, Cairns, and Tidman (1984) found significant linear declines with age in each of five SDQ scales, a significant nonlinear effect in Peer Relations, and no age effect in Parent Relations (which remained consistently high across grades).

Differing somewhat from the results of Marsh, Barnes, Cairns, and Tidman (1984), data from the Normative Archive SDQ Sample (which includes Sample G among many others), yielded a significant linear age effect for Peer Relations and Parent Relations as well as for the five other scales (Marsh, 1985).

Marsh, Barnes, Cairns, and Tidman (1984) suggest that decline of self-concept reports with age is consonant with the idea that children acquire more comparative information as they get older, leading to a decline in what originally may have been unrealistically high self-concepts.

In accordance with Shavelson's theory that self-concept facets become more differentiated with age is the fact that the median correlation among factors decreases across grade levels 2, 3, 4, 5, thus: .27, .19, .18, .14. No significance tests are available for this sequence, however.

Family/school socioeconomic level (SES). For students attending high SES schools, self-concept scores from the Reading, Mathematics, and All School Subjects scales correlated positively and significantly with family SES, whereas correlations between family SES and nonacademic self-concept scores were negligible. This suggests the discriminant validity of the academic and nonacademic scales. No partial *r*s are given to show whether the correlations between family SES and academic self-concept scores hold true if individual academic ability/achievement levels are held constant.

For students attending low SES schools, none of the correlations between family SES and self-concept scores was significant.

Finally, as predicted by reference-group theory, students from low SES schools (where the academic ability and achievement of the reference group is lower) had higher mean academic self-concept scores than did students from high SES schools (where academic ability and achievement of the reference group is higher). This held true at each of three levels of individual family SES (Marsh, 1984b; Marsh & Parker, 1984, both using Sample B).

Exceptions to the Shavelson model. Although the SDQ was designed to test the Shavelson model, and though results obtained with it have supported this model in several respects, the unexpected near-zero correlation between Mathematics self-concept and Reading self-concept scores failed to support the model.

Marsh, Smith, and Barnes (1985) attempt to explain the lack of correlation by positing that each student develops a mathematics self-concept and a reading self-concept not only by comparison with others' performances (external frame of reference that should yield positive correlations between Mathematics and Reading self-concepts, since mathematics and reading achievement scores are correlated), but also by taking note of the difference between his or her own performance in mathematics and reading (internal frame of reference that should yield negative correlations between mathematics self-concept scores and reading self-concept scores). (See also Marsh, 1986b, for relevant analyses involving all three SDQ instruments.)

Marsh and Shavelson (1985, Sample G) have used confirmatory factor analysis to test a number of models that take into account the lack of predicted correlation between Mathematics and Reading self-concepts coupled with the correlation of each with the General School self-concept. The model favored by their results posits two second-order academic factors (Reading Academic and Mathematics Academic) with the General School factor loading on each, and a second-order nonacademic factor. The Parent Relations factor is allowed to load on each of the two second-order academic factors. They conclude, "This model is consistent with Shavelson's assumption that self-concept is hierarchically ordered, but the particular form of this higher-order structure is more complicated than previously proposed" (p. 115).

8

SELF-DESCRIPTION QUESTIONNAIRE II (SDQ II)

(Marsh, in press b)

Rationale and General Description

The Self-Description Questionnaire II (SDQ II),[1] for use with adolescent respondents, is designed to measure 11 facets of self-concept, in accordance with Shavelson, Hubner, and Stanton's (1976) model. These facets, which correspond to some extent with those purportedly measured by the SDQ and the SDQ III, are as follows: General Self (modified Rosenberg Self-Esteem Scale), Mathematics, Verbal, General School, Physical Abilities, Physical Appearance, Same Sex Peer Relations, Opposite Sex Peer Relations, Parent Relations, Honesty, and Emotional Stability.

Item/Scale Selection and Refinement

There is some overlap with the SDQ in content areas and items, and some items have been added purporting to cover new content areas—that is, Emotional Stability, Honesty, Same Sex Peer Relations, and Opposite Sex Peer Relations. To what extent the actual items are the same for the SDQ II, SDQ, and SDQ III cannot be determined from published sources.

An original pool of 153 items was gradually reduced by unpublished item-analytic techniques to 140, then to 122 (used

---

1. The SDQ II is newer than the SDQ or SDQ III, so considerably less research has been done with it thus far.

by Marsh, Parker, & Barnes, 1985), and finally to 102 recommended by the current manual (Marsh, in press b) but not as yet used in published research.

Each of the 11 scales contains 8 or 10 items, half being negatively worded. No research basis is published to support the inclusion of negative items (in contrast to their exclusion from the SDQ), but Marsh (personal communication, April 22, 1988) indicates that preliminary research has suggested that negative item bias is not a problem in the age group for which SDQ II is intended.

Each item is responded to on a 6-point scale, ranging from False to True.

Factor analytically derived scale scores were correlated with respective raw scale scores, yielding a median r of .986.

Since the median intrascale correlation between the 122- and 102-item versions is .994 (Marsh, in press b), new research should be comparable with the work already published.

Samples

In four articles and a manual, Marsh and his colleagues report on several samples, all from metropolitan Sydney, Australia. (The letter designations are ones I assigned.)

Sample J

$N = 901$, 47% female, 7th to 12th graders, ages 11–18, enrolled in one public school in a mostly middle- and working-class city near Sydney; IQ mean = 101.6, SD = 13.4 (Marsh, Parker, & Barnes, 1985).

Sample K

$N = 962$, 49% female, 7th to 11th graders, enrolled in one of two middle-class suburban schools near Sydney during Year 2 of a study of transition from single-sex to coeducational schools. Sample K (Marsh, 1987a) is a subset of Sample N described below.

Sample L
$N = 130$, 79 boys and 51 girls, attending ninth grade in sex-segregated high schools in metropolitan Sydney (Thomas, 1984, cited in Marsh, in press b).

Sample M
$N = 137$ eighth-grade girls attending Catholic school in metropolitan Sydney (Marsh & Peart, in press).

Sample N
$N =$ approximately 3,073, percentage female unspecified, grades 7–11, enrolled in sex-segregated schools, then in coeducational schools in a 4-year longitudinal study (Marsh, Smith, Myers, & Owens, in press). Sample N includes Sample K.

Normative Archive SDQ II Sample
Normative data given in the forthcoming manual (Marsh, in press b) are based on 5,494 sets of *responses* from the approximately 3,073 individuals of Sample N. The number of different individuals is unspecifiable owing to repeated testing and necessary omission of identifying information (H. Marsh, personal communication, April 22, 1988).

Although they include many male and female subjects from varying educational, socioeconomic, and religious backgrounds, the samples are restricted with respect to geographical location, urbanness, and ethnicity. Accordingly, the generalizability of the reported findings, although plausible, remains to be demonstrated.

Descriptive Statistics

In the forthcoming SDQ II manual (Marsh, in press b), means, standard deviations, and indices of skew are given for the raw scores of the 5,494 *responses* from the Normative Archive SDQ II Sample and 2,658 male responses and 2,836 female responses from this sample. It is apparent that the score distribution for each scale is extremely skewed.

Reliability

Internal Consistency
For the 122-item version, alpha coefficients varied between .78 and .90 (median = .86) (Marsh, Parker, & Barnes, 1985, Sample J).

Alpha coefficients from the Normative Archive SDQ II Sample and the 102-item version are Verbal, .86; Mathematics, .90; General School, .87; Physical Abilities, .85; Appearance, .91; Opposite Sex Relations, .90; Same Sex Relations, .86; Honesty, .84; Parent Relations, .87; Emotional Stability, .84; General Self (Esteem), .88.

Test-Retest
The only stability data come from Sample M (137 eighth-grade girls) for whom the 7-week test-retest coefficients were as follows: Verbal, .85; Mathematics, .88; General School, .82; Physical Abilities, .86; Appearance, .75; Opposite Sex Relations, .79; Same Sex Relations, .76; Parent Relations, .77; Honesty, .73; Emotional Stability, .72; General Self (Esteem), .85.

Construct Validity

Factor-Analytic Checks on Dimensionality
Marsh (in press, b) reports "Many factor analyses of responses to SDQ II by diverse populations of subjects of different ages have each identified the 11 hypothesized factors" (p. 3). However, only two factor analyses have been published—one by Marsh, Parker, and Barnes (1985, Sample J), and one based on the 5,494 responses in the Normative Archive SDQ II Sample (Marsh, in press b).

For reasons explained in the discussion of the SDQ above, the factor analyses were based on item pairs rather than on individual items. Marsh (in press b) summarizes the larger factor analysis as follows:

The factor loadings for variables designed to measure each factor, the target loadings, are substantial, ranging from 0.48 [for one pair of All

School Subjects items] to 0.80 [for one pair of Mathematics items] (median = 0.68). The non-target loadings range from −0.12 to 0.27 (median = 0.03). The correlations among the factors are modest, ranging from −.03 to 0.39 (median = 0.15). (p. 11)

The correlation between Mathematics and Verbal self-concept factors is negligible (.03), in this respect failing to fulfill the original Shavelson model but in line with the revision of this model proposed by Marsh and Shavelson (1985).

Marsh and Smith (1987) have argued, "Unless factor structures are similar, there may be no basis for comparing mean differences [e.g., between sex, age, or nationality groups]" (p. 62). Although no formal explorations of factorial invariance across samples have been published, Marsh has computed separate factor analyses on younger and older subjects and on male and female subjects from the Normative Archive SDQ II Sample. Within each subgroup, factor scores derived from that group's factor analysis were very highly correlated with factor scores derived from the factor analysis from the total Normative Archive SDQ II Sample, supporting invariance across sex and age (H. Marsh, personal communication, May 26, 1988).

Irrelevant Response/Score Determiners
The following, with their attendant threats to validity, were avoided: forced-choice format, dichotomous scoring, item overlap between scales (except between scale scores and total scores), ipsative scoring, and two-part indices (discrepancy scores).

In contrast to the SDQ, half the items are negative, half positive, presumably providing some control of acquiescent response set. The data used for the norm tables were collected anonymously and under conditions that would entail no need to be dishonest.

In addition, Marsh and his associates argue that the distinct patterns of correlations obtained ("clean" factor patterns) and the absence of a general factor militate against the idea that important influences of acquiescent response set and social-desirability bias affect their self-concept scores.

No attempt has been made to evaluate (and if necessary to circumvent) the possibility that at least some of the "low self-concept" scores might represent unreliable responding due to lack of understanding, inattention, or uncooperativeness, as opposed to validly representing a poor self-evaluation. This problem needs to be considered, since for each scale the distribution is very skewed. (See above, under the SDQ, for details about this issue.)

Convergent and Discriminant Validity

Convergent validity coefficients and multitrait-multimethod matrices. Although several complex studies have been done using the SDQ II, neither convergent validity coefficients nor multitrait-multimethod analyses are available for this instrument. This is a very serious gap in the information needed to evaluate the construct validity of the SDQ II.

Under the heading Assumed Validity below, some studies are discussed in which self-concept scale scores are differently related to other variables, for example, to sex or achievement. However, this is the only information of possible relevance to the discriminant construct validity of this instrument. What is known about the convergent and discriminant validity of the SDQ II contrasts markedly with the state of knowledge about the SDQ.

Since the SDQ II is the most recently devised of the three Self-Description Questionnaires, needed information about its convergent and discriminant validity will be forthcoming.

Assumed Validity Studies

When self-concept scores are found to be related to other variables in a manner predicted by theory, the construct validity of the self-concept scores is supported, albeit not unequivocally.

A number of the studies cited below related SDQ II scores to other variables, and I have also included some that were not based on a priori predictions.

As with the SDQ, these studies focus mainly on the relationships between the academic self-concept scores of the SDQ II and other variables. Thus, much remains to be done to explore the construct validity of the other self-concept scales by means of "assumed validity studies."

Academic achievement indicators and study skills. In Sample

L, Thomas 1984 (cited in Marsh, in press b) found significant correlations between the *mathematical ability groupings* of subjects and their Verbal, Mathematics, and All School Subjects Scores, supporting assumptions about the validity of these academic self-concept scales. However, significant *r*s were also found between mathematics ability groupings and Same Sex Peer Relations and Honesty self-concepts, thus weakening the implied support of the overall pattern of results for the discriminant validity of the self-concept scales.

A *study skills inventory* of undescribed psychometric properties correlated significantly with 9 out of 11 self-concept scales, which is not what one would expect if both instruments have discriminant validity for academic-related constructs. Similarly, the "deep" and "achieving" dimensions of a Survey of Study Processes correlated significantly with the same 9 out of 11 self-concept scales, which again is not what one would expect if both instruments have discriminant validity for academic-related constructs.

From Sample M, Marsh and Peart (in press) obtained significant correlations between subjects' *assigned mathematics ability groupings* and their self-concept scores on Verbal (.27), Mathematics (.48), and All School Subjects (.50) scales. Although three other significant correlations were also obtained (Parent Relations, .22; Honesty, .23; and General Esteem, .23), they are smaller than those between achievement and the academic self-concept scales, thereby giving some visual support to the discriminant validity of the academic self-concept scales.

Marsh, Parker, and Barnes (1985, Sample J), correlated subjects' assigned *English ability* and *mathematics ability groupings* with each of the 11 SDQ II scales in each grade 7 through 11/12 (except that no mathematical ability groupings were available for seventh graders). The correlations of English groupings versus Verbal self-concept and versus All School Subjects were usually the highest of any correlations involving English groupings, ranging from .13 to .35. Also, correlations of mathematical ability groupings versus Mathematics self-concepts and versus All School Subjects self-concepts were usually the highest of any correlations involving mathematical ability groupings, ranging from .16 to .45. English ability groupings correlated better with Verbal self-concept scores than with Mathematics self-concept scores, and mathematical ability groupings correlated better with Mathematics self-concept scores than with Verbal self-concept scores.

Overall, the pattern in these data offers support for the discriminant validity of the academic self-concept scales of the SDQ II.

Age effects. As already discussed in the section on the SDQ, Marsh, Barnes, Cairns, and Tidman (1984) found a significant decline in SDQ scores across grade levels 2–5, except for the Parent Relations scale. In commenting on this finding, Marsh, Parker, and Barnes (1985) remark:

Marsh proposed a social comparison process whereby the added experience and reality testing gained by attending school causes the high reported self-concepts of very young children (perhaps unrealistically high when the average response is nearly 4.5 on a 5-point response scale) to drop, but has no effect on the Parents scale where children have no external basis of comparison. Thus, preadolescent children still feel confident about their relationship with their parents even after they find they are not as good as they once thought in other areas. He also predicted that the extremely high self-concepts on the Parent scale were unlikely to be maintained through the adolescent years. (p. 424)

However, with the exception of the Parent Relations scale, this prediction does not state whether or on what basis age effects might be reasonably expected in the SDQ II responses from subjects in grades 7–12. Thus, their findings from SDQ II responses may not, strictly speaking, be considered relevant to the assumed validity of the SDQ II.

Marsh and Smith (1987) argue that mean age differences may not be interpretable unless factor structures are invariant across age. As explained above, Marsh has presented evidence of factorial invariance across age, promoting the interpretability of mean differences between age groups.

Finally, caution is in order when interpreting age effects obtained from a cross-sectional design.

With the considerations above in mind, the following age effects are presented.

In a study by Marsh, Parker, and Barnes (1985), using Sample J (901 boys and girls from grades 7–12 in one coeducational school), the following scales yielded significant quadratic age effects whereby self-concept scores were highest in grades 7, 11, and 12 and lowest in grade 9: General Self (Esteem), Mathematics, Verbal, All School Subjects, Physical Abilities, Same Sex Relations, Honesty, and Total score. Age effects were primarily linear for the Opposite Sex Relations scale (self-concept scores increasing with age) and for the Parent Relations scale (self-concept scores decreasing with age). Emotional Stability showed no age effect.

Marsh, Smith, Myers, and Owens (in press) present Total self-concept data for Sample N, including 948 students (percentage female unspecified) in grades 7–11 of sex-segregated schools. The lowest total self-concept means were in grades 9 and 10, as was true for the total score and six of the separate scales in the Marsh, Parker, and Barnes (1985) study. Because data for separate scales are not presented by Marsh, Smith, Myers, and Owens (in press), scale-by-scale comparisons of age effects found in each of the two studies cannot be made.

Failing to support the Shavelson model, adolescent self-concepts did not become more distinct with age, as evidenced by the following median interscale correlations of factor scores for grades 7 through 11/12: .12, .17, .18, .17, .17 (Marsh, Parker, & Barnes, 1985).

Sex differences. As discussed above, Marsh and his colleagues (Marsh, Smith, & Barnes, 1983; Marsh, Relich, & Smith, 1983) expected to find gender differences on separate scales of SDQ, according to sex stereotypes. Specifically, boys were expected to have higher self-concepts on the Physical Abilities and Mathematics scales, girls to have higher self-concepts in Reading (and these predictions were largely borne out, as stated in the discussion of the SDQ above). However, Marsh (in press b) and Marsh, Parker, and Barnes (1985) made no definite predictions about sex effects for the SDQ II in the data for Sample J (grades 7–12). Thus, their findings from these SDQ II responses may not, strictly speaking, be considered relevant to the assumed validity of the SDQ II.

As explained above, Marsh has presented evidence of factorial invariance of SDQ II scores across gender, justifying the interpretability of mean differences between the sexes.

With these considerations in mind, the following sex differences are presented: Boys scored signficantly higher on General Self (Esteem), Mathematics, Physical Abilities, Appearance, and Emotional Stability scales. Girls scored significantly higher on Verbal, Same Sex Relations, and Honesty scales. No significant sex differences were found on the Opposite Sex Relations, Parent Relations, or All School Subjects scales. No age by sex interactions were found (Marsh, Parker, & Barnes, 1985, Sample J).

Marsh, Smith, Myers, and Owens (in press) obtained a significant sex effect favoring boys when considering the combined scores from all 12 scales (including the Total score) and four testing times in a repeated-measures analysis. The within-subject comparisons showed that the effect of sex differed depending on the area of self-concept. These effects were very small, however.

Combining the data from each of two times (before and after transition to coeducational schools), they found that females' scores were significantly higher on the *Verbal*, Academic, *Same Sex Relations*, Parent Relations, and *Honesty* scales, whereas males' scores were significantly higher on the *Mathematics, Physical Abilities, Appearance*, Opposite Sex Relations, *Emotional Stability*, and *General Self (Esteem)* scales. (The findings for the scales listed in italics replicate those reported by Marsh, Parker, & Barnes, 1985.)

Physical fitness. As they predicted, Marsh and Peart (in press) found that performance on seven physical fitness tests correlated significantly with Physical Ability self-concept scores, but not with any other SDQ II scores in a sample of 137 girls (Sample M).

9

SELF-DESCRIPTION
QUESTIONNAIRE III (SDQ III)
(Marsh, in press c)

Rationale and General Description

The Self-Description Questionnaire III (SDQ III), intended for
late adolescent and young adult respondents, is based on Shavelson, Hubner, and Stanton's (1976) model and on previous research with the SDQ, discussed above.

It is a purported measure of 13 factors of self-concept:
Mathematics, Verbal, Academic, Problem Solving/Creativity,
Physical Abilities/Sports, Physical Appearance, Same Sex Peer
Relations, Opposite Sex Peer Relations, Parent Relations, Religion/Spirituality, Honesty/Reliability, Emotional Stability/Security, and General Self (Esteem). The items are given in Appendix I of Marsh and O'Neill (1984).

Six of the SDQ scales were retained in the SDQ III: Mathematics, Verbal, Academic, Physical Abilities/Sports, Physical
Appearance, and Parent Relations. The seventh (Peer Relations)
was made into two scales (Same Sex Peer Relations and Opposite
Sex Peer Relations). Four scales were added, following suggestions by respondents to a preliminary version of the SDQ III:
Problem Solving/Creativity, Religion/Spirituality, Honesty/
Reliability, and Emotional Stability/Security. The authors also
included a 13th (General Self [Esteem]) scale, a modification of
Rosenberg's Self-Esteem Scale. (Marsh, Barnes, & Hocevar
[1985] believe that these facets of self-concept do not exhaust
those that "must surely exist [and must be] quite important to a
few individuals" [p. 1363].)

Item/Scale Selection and Refinement

A succession of unpublished item analyses and factor analyses led to the selection of 136 items, each of the 13 SDQ III scales being represented by 10 or 12 items. Each item is responded to on an 8-point scale from Definitely False to Definitely True. Approximately half the items in each scale are worded positively, half negatively. The inclusion of negative items in the SDQ III (in contrast to their exclusion from the SDQ) was justified by three lines of evidence: (1) Preliminary factor analyses and item analyses indicated that the inclusion of negative items was justified. (2) Convergent validity coefficients between SDQ III scores and subjects' self-concepts as inferred by others did not differ according to whether they were based on positively or negatively worded SDQ III items. (3) Test-retest coefficients involving a one-month interval did not vary according to whether they were based on positively or negatively worded SDQ III items (Marsh, in press c).

The complete set of items appears in Marsh and O'Neill (1984, Appendix I).

Samples

Information about SDQ III comes from 2,410 sets of responses representing 1,202 different urban Australian individuals and from 991 persons from Ottawa, Canada. Each sample was used in more than one study; therefore, to save repetition later on, I describe each sample immediately below, labeling each by a letter or name for ready reference. Samples Q, R, S_a and S_b responded to only four SDQ III scales.

Sample O
N = 296 females, grade 11, mean age 16.2, Catholic school (Marsh, 1986a; Marsh & O'Neill, 1984; Marsh & Shavelson, 1985).

Sample P
N = 151, 76 females and 75 males, Australian college and university students (Marsh, 1986a; Marsh, 1986b; Marsh, Barnes, & Hocevar, 1985; Marsh & O'Neill, 1984).

The 76 females used by Marsh and Jackson (1986) constitute Sample P'.

Sample Q

N = 30 female powerlifters (Jackson & Marsh, 1986; Marsh, 1986a; Marsh & Jackson, 1986).

Sample R

N = 991 students in grades 11 and 12; 457 females and 516 males, Ottawa, Canada (Byrne, in press a; Byrne, in press b; Byrne & Shavelson, 1986; Byrne & Shavelson, 1987; Marsh, Byrne, & Shavelson, in press).

Sample S_a

N = 46 female athletes, grades 10–12 in private school, mean age 16.7; high academic ability, upper-middle class (Jackson & Marsh, 1986; Marsh, 1986a; Marsh & Jackson, 1986).

Sample S_b

N = 46 female nonathletes, grades 10–12 in private school, mean age 16.7; high academic ability, upper-middle class (Marsh, 1986a; Marsh & Jackson, 1986).

Sample T

N = 361, 24% female, ages 16–31 (median = 21), 96% single, Outward Bound participants. Sample T was tested four times over a 20-month period (Marsh, 1986a; Marsh, 1986b; Marsh, 1987c; Marsh & Richards, [in press a, 280 members of Sample T]; Marsh, Richards, & Barnes, 1986a; Marsh, Richards, & Barnes, 1986b).

Normative Archive SDQ III Sample

N = 2,410 *responses* from 1,202 individuals aged 15 and older, largely comprising Samples O through Q and Sample T (Marsh, in press c; Marsh, in review).

The total number of subjects used in developing the SDQ III is considerably smaller than the number used in developing the SDQ and SDQ II, and "the representativeness of the normative base for the SDQ III . . . is more dubious" (Marsh, in review, p. 11), since the samples tend to overrepresent males, students, and persons under 26 years of age. The generalizability of the data across different national, ethnic, and social groups remains to be determined.

Descriptive Statistics

The forthcoming manual for the SDQ III (Marsh, in press c) gives means and SDs for each item for the Normative Archive SDQ III Sample. Also given for the same sample are means, medians, SDs, and indices of skew for each self-concept scale. A marked skew toward the unfavorable end of the score range is apparent for each self-concept scale.

Most of the studies done thus far have been based on SDQ III factor scores rather than raw scores because "factor analytically derived scores distinguish better among the SDQ III facets than do the unweighted scale scores, and they are more clearly related to various criterion measures" (Marsh, in press c, p. 8). Factor scores are produced by the author's computer scoring program based on the normative sample, or users may obtain factor scores based on their own samples, employing the author's computer scoring program.

Reliability

Internal Consistency
Alpha reliabilities for each scale appear in Marsh and O'Neill (1984, Sample O), in Marsh, Barnes, and Hocevar (1985, Sample P), and in Marsh (in press c) for the Normative Archive SDQ III Sample as well as for Times 1, 2, 3, and 4 of Sample T. The ranges of these alpha coefficients are Mathematics, .93 to .95; Verbal, .84 to .88; Academic, .85 to .92; Problem Solving, .77 to .84; Physical Abilities, .92 to .96; Appearance, .86 to .90; Same Sex Peer Relations, .81 to .91; Opposite Sex Peer Relations, .90 to .93; Parent Relations, .87 to .91; Religious/Spiritual, .89 to .95; Honesty, .72 to .75; Emotional Stability, .89 to .91; General Self (Esteem), .93 to .94.

A Canadian sample (Sample R) responded to only four scales with the following reliabilities: Mathematics, .92, English (Verbal), .79; Academic, .89, and General Self (Esteem), .93 (Byrne & Shavelson, 1986).

Test-Retest

The only test-retest information available is based on some subjects from Sample T (229 of the 361 Outward Bound participants): for 1 month, the range is from .76 for Honesty to .94 for Mathematics (median = .87); for 2 months, the range is from .63 for Honesty to .93 for Religion (median = .83); for 20 months, the range is from .49 for Honesty to .87 for Mathematics (median = .73).

Construct Validity

Factor-Analytic Checks on Dimensionality

All extant factor analyses of the 13 scales are based on item pairs, not on individual items, for reasons explained in the SDQ section of this book.

The first fully published factor analysis involving the 13 scales (Marsh & O'Neill, 1984, Sample O) yielded 13 clearly identified first-order factors. Because the correlations among factors were very low (mean = .08) and not even the General Self (Esteem) factor correlated substantially with the other factors, the "findings strongly suggest no hierarchical structure underlies the 13 SDQ III factors" (p. 160), failing to support the Shavelson model.

Although factor tables are not published, summary results for Sample P are given in Marsh and O'Neill (1984) and in Marsh, Barnes, and Hocevar (1985). Median target loading = .67 (range .23 to .92). Median nontarget loading = .02 (range −.28 to .43). Median correlation among oblique factors = .07 (range −.19 to .32).

Somewhat modifying the provisional conclusions of Marsh and O'Neill, Marsh, Barnes, and Hocevar (1985) conclude, "The small correlations among the factors demonstrate that they are relatively independent and that any hierarchical structure underlying the factors must be very weak" (p. 1365).

The forthcoming SDQ III manual (Marsh, in press c) presents results of confirmatory factor analyses of the data from the Normative Archive SDQ III Sample. The results give partial support to the revised Marsh/Shavelson model. As predicted, correlations among the four academic factors and among the eight nonacademic factors generally exceed those between academic and nonacademic factors. Correlations among academic factors support the two second-order academic factors posited in the Marsh/Shavelson revised model. On the other hand, correlations among the nonacademic factors do not clearly support the expected second-order nonacademic factors (physical, social, moral). (The testing and evaluation of various revised models is discussed in Marsh, in press c. See also Marsh, 1987c.)

Tabulating information across each of nine published and unpublished factor analyses including all those above, Marsh (in press c) reports the following: 68 target loadings range from .23 to .96; 716 nontarget loadings range from −.28 to .43; 78 factor correlations range from −.19 to .41. This set of summary data does not permit any overall statement about the relevance of the entire set to the Shavelson model.

Marsh and Smith (1987) have argued that "unless the factor structures are similar, there may be no basis for comparing mean differences [e.g., between sex, age, or nationality groups]" (p. 62). Although no formal explorations of factorial invariance across samples have been published, Marsh has computed separate factor analyses on younger and older subjects and on male and female subjects from the Normative Archive SDQ III Sample. Within each subgroup, factor scores derived from that group's factor analysis were very highly correlated with factor scores derived from the factor analysis from the total Normative Archive SDQ III Sample, supporting invariance across sex and age (H. Marsh, personal communication, May 26, 1988).

Besides the extant factor analyses on all 13 SDQ III scales, Byrne and Shavelson (1986) summarize their item-level factor analytic results from Sample R, who responded to only the General Self (Esteem), Mathematics, English, and Academic self-concept scales. They say only that four clearly defined factors emerged, accounting for 48%, 26.7%, 16.6%, and 8.7% of the variance; 41 out of 42 items loaded .34 or more on the target factors, and correlations among factors ranged from .07 to .36 (mean = .22). Five items from the Academic scale yielded results not fully congruent with the hierarchical model. "Although the number of factors, pattern of factor loadings (except one) and hierarchical structure were invariant across gender, relations among the factors differed" (Byrne and Shavelson, 1987, p. 365). (See under Sex Effects below.)

In a factorial study of item pairs, also using Sample R and the four SDQ III scales, General Self (Esteem), Mathematics, English, and Academic, Byrne (in press b) found equivalency of structure across two academic tracks (high and low).

Irrelevant Response/Score Determiners

The following, with their attendant threats to validity, were avoided: forced-choice format, dichotomous scoring, item ambiguity, item overlap between scales (except between scale scores and total scores), ipsative scoring, and two-part indices (discrepancy scores).

In contrast to the SDQ, half the items are negative, half positive, presumably providing some control of acquiescent response set.

In addition, Marsh and his associates argue that the distinct patterns of correlations obtained ("clean" factor patterns) and the absence of a general factor militate against the idea that important influences of acquiescent response set and social-desirability bias affect their self-concept scores.

No attempt has been made to evaluate (and if necessary to circumvent) the possibility that at least some of the "low self-concept" scores might represent unreliable responding due to lack of understanding, inattention, or uncooperativeness, as opposed to validly representing a poor self-evaluation. This problem needs to be considered, since for each scale the distribution is very skewed. (See above, under the SDQ, for details about this issue.)

Convergent and Discriminant Validity
Convergent validity coefficients. Marsh, Smith, and Barnes (1983) have suggested that using various forms of self-concept self-reports as a means for evaluating construct validity really amounts to obtaining reliability measures. Nevertheless, one type of convergent validity measure used by Marsh and O'Neill (1984, Sample O) and by Marsh, Barnes, and Hocevar (1985, Sample P) was the correlation between each SDQ III scale and the subjects' self-ratings on 13 corresponding single-rating scales. The convergent validity coefficients from the two samples were Mathematics, .76, .86; Verbal, .47, .59; Academic, .51, .63; Problem Solving, .57, .56; Physical Abilities, .79, .82; Appearance, .65, .54; Same Sex Peer Relations, .46, .64; Opposite Sex Peer Relations, .76, .74; Parent Relations, .73, .82; Religion/Spirituality, .73, .90; Honesty/Reliability, .33, .50; Emotional Stability, .47, .66.

For the four SDQ III scales they used with Sample R, Byrne and Shavelson (1987) give the following convergent validity coefficients between SDQ III scales and other purportedly corresponding self-report scales.

1. SDQ III General Self (Esteem) scale versus Self-Concept subscales of Soares and Soares (1979) Affective Perception Inventory (API), .63, and versus Rosenberg's (1965) Self-Esteem Scale, .79.
2. SDQ III Academic self-concept versus API Student Self, .62, and versus Brookover's (1962) Self-Concept of Ability Scale (SCA) Form A, .68.
3. SDQ III Verbal self-concept versus API English Perceptions subscale, .71, and versus Brookover's SCA Form B, .54.
4. SDQ III Mathematics self-concept versus API Mathematics Perceptions subscale, .86, and versus Brookover's SCA Form C, .83.

In a study of the construct dimensions possibly represented by the 90 items of the Tennessee Self-Concept Scale (TSCS; Fitts, 1965), Marsh and Richards (in press a, Sample T), using a variety of factor-analytic approaches, obtained clear support only for the differentiation among the Physical, Social, and Family scales of the TSCS. These three scales seem conceptually comparable to certain SDQ III scales, so the following may be considered validity coefficients.

TSCS Physical versus SDQ III Physical Abilities, .53.
TSCS Physical versus SDQ III Appearance, .71.
TSCS Social versus SDQ III Same Sex Peer Relations, .61.
TSCS Social versus SDQ III Opposite Sex Peer Relations, .59.
TSCS Family versus SDQ III Parent Relations, .68.

(All the convergent validity coefficients above exceeded the correlations between these scales and noncorresponding TSCS scales, thereby offering some support to the discriminant validity of these SDQ III scales.)

A stronger test of convergent validity is afforded by the coefficients between each SDQ III scale and the corresponding inferences about the respondents' self-concepts made by others who knew them well (Marsh & O'Neill, 1984; Marsh, Barnes, & Hocevar, 1985, both Sample P; Marsh & Richards, in press a, 280 members of Sample T). These coefficients are Mathematics, .77, .42; Verbal, .51, .31; Academic, .31, .44; Problem Solving, .52, .28; Physical Abilities, .78, .49; Appearance, .50, .32; Same Sex Peer Relations, .45, .26; Opposite Sex Peer Relations, .51, .45; Parent Relations, .76, .37; Religion/Spirituality, .79, .57; Honesty/Reliability, .44, .26; Emotional Stability, .62, .17; General Self (Esteem), .46, —. (With few exceptions in both data sets, these coefficients exceeded cross-correlations involving external observers' ratings of one dimension and subjects' self-concept scores on another dimension, supporting the discriminant validity of SDQ III scores. See the multitrait-multimethod results for Sample P, below.)

Multitrait-multimethod matrices. Marsh and O'Neill (1984, Sample O) present a multitrait-multimethod matrix for 13 variables measured by two methods—SDQ III and summary self-ratings. In support of the convergent and discriminant validity of the SDQ III scales, they report the following pattern for the SDQ III:

1. Reliability of SDQ III (mean monotrait-monomethod), $r = .80$.
2. Convergent validity (mean monotrait-heteromethod), $r = .60$.
3. Heterotrait-monomethod (different traits by same self-report

method), mean r for SDQ III $= .08$, mean r for self-ratings $= .15$.

4. Heterotrait-heteromethod (SDQ III vs. self-ratings across different traits), mean $r = .09$.

Marsh and O'Neill (1984, Sample P) also present a multi-trait-multimethod matrix for 13 variables measured by the SDQ III and by others' inferences about the respondents' self-concepts. In support of the convergent and discriminant validity of the SDQ III scales, they report the following pattern for the SDQ III:

1. Reliability of SDQ III (mean monotrait-monomethod), $r = .88$.
2. Convergent validity (mean monotrait-heteromethod), $r = .58$.
3. Heterotrait-monomethod rs (different traits by the same self-report method): for 310 out of 312 comparisons, these rs are smaller than the convergent validity coefficients.
4. Heterotrait-heteromethod rs (SDQ III vs. others' inferences across different traits): in 312 out of 312 comparisons, these rs are smaller than the convergent validity coefficients.

Byrne and Shavelson (1986) present a multitrait-multimethod matrix for Sample R, using only four self-concept constructs (general esteem, academic self-concept, mathematics self-concept, and verbal self-concept), each measured by each of three different self-report instruments: SDQ III, Soares and Soares's (1979) Affective Perception Inventory, Brookover's (1962) Self-Concept of Ability Scales (for the academic constructs only), and Rosenberg's (1965) Self-Esteem Scale for the General Esteem construct. Considering the SDQ III correlations, one sees an order that is visually supportive of the convergent and discriminant validity of the SDQ III, namely:

1. Reliability of SDQ III (mean monotrait-monomethod), $r = .88$.
2. Convergent validity (mean monotrait-heteromethod), $r = .71$.
3. Heterotrait-monomethod (different traits by the SDQ III method), mean $r = .27$.
4. Heterotrait-heteromethod (SDQ III scales vs. noncorresponding scales from API, SCAS, or RSE), mean $r = .27$.

The results from the three multitrait-multimethod matrices are visually supportive of the convergent and discriminant validity of the SDQ III scales. The matrix offering the strongest support for the convergent and discriminant validity of each of the 13 SDQ III scales is Marsh and O'Neill's matrix for Sample P, because it uses non-self-report data as the validity criterion for each scale and shows that more than 99% of the comparisons between convergent validity coefficients and heterotrait-monomethod and heterotrait-heteromethod correlations fulfill Campbell and Fiske's (1959) criteria.

Of course even such favorable multitrait-multimethod data cannot tell how large the difference between an individual's two scale scores must be in order to indicate a reliable intraindividual difference between two self-concept facets.

Assumed Validity

Studies in this category are based on the assumptions that the psychometric scale in question validly indexes a designated construct and that a stated relationship obtains between the construct measured by the scale and one or more other variables.

Some of the studies described below do not make the second assumption but are included here for their value in exploring the relations between SDQ III scales and other variables.

Virtually all the studies relating SDQ III scores to other variables in order to test theory-based predictions involve only the three academic self-concept scales. Almost everything remains to be done to explore the construct validity of the other 10 SDQ III scales by using them to test theory-based predictions.

Intellectual and academic variables. Two studies have supported the expectations that SDQ III Mathematics self-concept scores would correlate more highly with *mathematics achievement* than with English achievement and that SDQ III Verbal self-concept scores would correlate more highly with *English achievement* than with mathematics achievement (Byrne & Shavelson, 1986, Sample R; Marsh & O'Neill, 1984, Sample O).

One study (Marsh & O'Neill, 1984, Sample O), has supported the following expectations: (1) *Mathematics achievement* scores will correlate most highly with Mathematics self-concept, next most highly with Academic self-concept, and least (perhaps insignificantly) with Verbal self-concept. (2) *English achievement* scores will correlate most highly with Verbal self-concept, next most highly with Academic self-concept, and least with Mathematics self-concept. (3) Neither *English* nor *Mathematics achievement* scores will correlate with nonacademic scales of the SDQ III.

A second study relevant to the first two expectations used only the General Esteem, Academic, Mathematics, and Verbal scales of the SDQ III. Slightly differing versions of the relevant correlations are given in Byrne and Shavelson (1986, Sample R), and Marsh, Byrne, and Shavelson (in press, Sample R). However, in each version the first two expectations were fulfilled except that English achievement correlated more highly with Academic self-concept than with Verbal self-concept. Neither mathematics nor English achievement scores correlated with General Self (Esteem).

Age effects. Predictions were made that mean self-concept scores would increase across three age groups of the Normative Archive SDQ III Sample. These expectations stemmed as much from an overview of previous research as from theory. Accordingly, relations between age and SDQ III mean scores have somewhat limited relevance to the evaluation of the construct validity of the SDQ III (Marsh, in press c).

As explained above, Marsh has presented evidence of factorial invariance across age groups, justifying attempts to interpret age effects.

Age was significantly positively related to mean factor scores on the Verbal, Mathematics, Academic, Problem Solving, Physical Ability, Appearance, Honesty, Emotional Stability, and General Self (Esteem) scales. Significant negative relations obtained between age and mean factor scores on Same Sex Peer Relations and Religious/Spiritual scales (Marsh, in review, Normative Archive SDQ III Sample).

Contrary to the theoretical prediction of Shavelson, Hubner, and Stanton (1976) that the facets of self-concept become more differentiated with age, no change was observed in factor intercorrelations across the three age groups in the Normative Archive SDQ III Sample.

The usual limitations of cross-sectional studies may be

compounded here by the fact that the three age groups differed on other characteristics; for example, the youngest came mostly from a Catholic girls' school, the oldest mostly from university students and Outward Bound participants.

Sex effects. Sex effects were predicted to some extent on the basis of stereotypes and to some extent on the basis of previous research. Accordingly, sex effects have somewhat limited relevance to evaluating the construct validity of the SDQ III.

As explained above, Marsh has presented evidence of factorial invariance across sex groups, justifying attempts to interpret mean sex differences.

In the Normative Archive SDQ III Sample (Marsh, in review), females' mean factor scores significantly exceeded those of males on the Academic, Honesty, Religious/Spiritual, and Opposite Sex Peer Relations scales, whereas males exceeded females on Problem Solving, Mathematics, Physical Abilities, Appearance, Emotional Stability, and General Self (Esteem) scales. No sex differences were found on Verbal and Same Sex Peer Relations scales. The findings of higher male scores on Physical Appearance and no sex difference on Verbal self-concepts do not seem to follow sex stereotypes. The difference in Religious/Spiritual means may result because all Catholic-school subjects were females (who had higher Religious/Spiritual self-concepts than did other groups).

Byrne and Shavelson (1987), using only the Mathematics, Verbal, Academic, and General Self (Esteem) scales with Sample R, found that the number of self-concept factors and all but one factor loading followed a pattern that was invariant across gender. (SDQ III Mathematics loaded on the Verbal self-concept factor for males.)

Relations among the self-concept dimenions did show sex effects, however; for example, the General Self (Esteem) and Academic self-concept scores correlate more highly with Mathematics self-concept for males and with the English factor for females; for females, Verbal and Mathematics self-concepts correlated more highly with their corresponding grades than with grades in the other subject, but this was not true for males; the correlation between Verbal and Mathematics self-concept scores was low (but significant) for males, zero for females.

Parent relations. Rated satisfaction with the home environment correlated substantially with the Parent Relations self-concept scale and less strongly with the other self-concept scales (Marsh & O'Neill, 1984, Sample N).

Sports experience. It was expected that female sports experience would be associated with greater self-favorability on the Physical Abilities and Physical Appearance scales of the SDQ III (Jackson & Marsh, 1986, Samples Q, S_a and S_b; Marsh & Jackson, 1986, Samples P', Q, S_a and S_b.) According to the more complete report by Marsh and Jackson (1986), Physical Abilities scores and General Self (Esteem) scores but not Appearance scores were higher among athletes (Sample Q, young adult powerlifters, and Sample S_a, high-school athletes) than among nonathletes (Sample P', young adults, and Sample S_b, high-school students). Only four of the SDQ III scales were considered in this study.

Global self-esteem and specific self-concept facets. It seems plausible that SDQ III scale scores should correlate more highly with SDQ III General Self (Esteem) when scale scores are weighted according to their stated importance to each individual respondent. However, several statistical analyses relevant to this assumption failed to support the expectation (Marsh, 1986a).

Interventions. Marsh (in press c; Marsh, Richards, & Barnes, 1986a, 1986b) report on changes in SDQ III scores among Sample T subjects who participated in an Outward Bound course. The Outward Bound program director predicted that certain SDQ III scales (Mathematics, Academic, Opposite Sex Peer Relations, and Religion) would be less affected by participation than would the other SDQ III scales. Between Time 1 (one month before the program began) and Time 2 (Day 1 of the program), several significant decreases occurred, namely, in Academic, Problem Solving, Appearance, Physical Abilities, Honesty, and Emotional Stability scores. Between Time 2 and Time 3 (at the end of the program), mean scores in every scale increased significantly; and between Time 3 and Time 4 (18 months later), only three significant decreases occurred: in Parent Relations, Honesty, and Emotional Stability (Marsh, in press c; Marsh, Richards, & Barnes, 1986b).

The relevance of the total pattern of the three sets of changes to the construct validity of the SDQ III is unclear. Marsh (personal communication, May 26, 1988) reports that although all scale scores increased significantly between Times 2 and 3, "formal statistical tests comparing the sizes of changes in those scales predicted to be more and less affected . . . [showed that] those predicted to be more affected were more affected."

Also pertinent to interpreting the relevance of this study to the assumed validity of respective SDQ III scales is the absence of a control group. However, Marsh, Richards, and Barnes (1986b) present a long, detailed argument that the usual groups of this kind would not accomplish their intended purpose, are "unlikely to exist," or may not be feasible (Marsh, in press c).

Tests of the Internal/External (I/E) model. Verbal and mathematics achievement scores are positively correlated, and insofar as students' self-concepts are determined by these external sources of information, Verbal and Mathematics self-concept scores should also be positively correlated (in support of the Shavelson model). However, Verbal and Mathematics self-concepts are actually uncorrelated (Marsh, 1986b, SDQ III data from Samples O, P, T).

To explain this unexpected result, Marsh (1986b) suggests that each student's self-concepts in the mathematics and verbal areas are determined not only by knowledge of external achievement indicators but also by knowledge of which area is stronger for him or her. This internal frame of reference leads to an expectation of a negative correlation between Verbal and Mathematics self-concepts across students.

Thus, the combined effects of respondents' use of internal and external reference frames theoretically account for the negligible or zero correlations between Verbal and Mathematics self-concepts.

No student reports are available on whether they knowingly used both the information about their achievement scores and that about their relative achievement levels in the two areas when deciding on their responses to the Verbal and Mathematics self-concept scales.

(See the review of the SDQ above and Marsh, [1986b] for comparative information on the I/E model with reference to the SDQ and SDQ II tests.)

10

BODY CATHEXIS SCALE (BC) AND BODY ESTEEM SCALE (BES)

(Secord and Jourard, 1953;
Franzoi and Shields, 1984)

In my 1974 book, I reviewed Secord and Jourard's (1953) Body Cathexis Scale because it was among those involved in at least 12 studies; because it represented one of the various approaches to the scoring of self-evaluation (i.e., in terms of statements about self-acceptance rather than by using respondents' self-ideal discrepancies or implying that all respondents' ideals fall at the good end of each scale); and because it was the only scale purporting to measure that particular evaluative aspect of the self-concept, presumably important to overall self-regard yet conceptually distinct from it.

At that time, split-half reliabilities of .75 to .91 and a stability coefficient of .72 had been reported. There was no direct evidence about convergent validity, and there was some evidence of poor discriminant validity.

It seems intuitively obvious that self-evaluation of body parts and functions should be important in its own right, and on this assumption some recently used scales have included subscales relating to physical appearance, physical abilities, or both (e.g., SDQ, PH, and SPPC, reviewed in this book). However, Secord and Jourard's instrument, which is more specific and inclusive about aspects of the body, seems to have been used only rarely since 1972 (Balogun, 1986; Tucker, 1982).

Two recent factor analyses of it (Tucker, 1981; Hammond & O'Rourke, 1984) have led to different conclusions.

Since body evaluation still seems conceptually important,

and since the psychometric interpretability of the BC remains undemonstrated or questioned, I briefly discuss below a proposed revision of the scale (Body Esteem Scale) that may prove useful.

Rationale and General Description

Franzoi and Shields (1984) and Franzoi and Herzog (1986, 1987) have developed and used a three-subscale Body Esteem Scale (BES) based on the Body Cathexis Scale.

Item/Scale Selection and Refinement

The original BC items named 40 body parts and functions, each to be rated on a 5-point Likert scale from strong negative to strong positive feelings. Ratings are added across items to obtain a single score.

Two factor analyses of these items, one of 257 undergraduate males' responses, one of 366 undergraduate females' responses, indicated that body esteem is a multidimensional construct, with three factors for each gender.

The results of this factor analysis were used to construct a 39-item Body Esteem Scale by adding 16 new items on the basis of their assumed relevance to the three major factors and dropping 17 original BC items.

Responses to this 39-item version again yielded three factors, and after four low-loading items were dropped, reanalysis yielded three factors accounting for 39% of the male and 36% of the female total variance.

This 35-item version, published in both Franzoi and Shields (1984) and Franzoi and Herzog (1987), was used in a factor analysis of the responses of 331 male undergraduates and 633 female undergraduates, and the factor loadings of the items corresponded satisfactorily to those in the previous factor analyses. Two items for males had loadings of .35 or more on two factors (physical coordination and figure or physique).

According to criteria proposed by Harman (1967), it seemed appropriate to consider the three male factors different from the three female ones. The corresponding male/female subscales are named as follows: Physical Attractiveness/Sexual Attractiveness; Upper Body Strength/Weight Concern; Physical Condition/Physical Condition. Subscale correlations range from .33 to .65, with those for males higher than those for females.

Samples

It appears that a total of 1,283 females and 1,285 males, all undergraduates, have been used thus far in developing the BES. This homogeneity in age and educational level obviously limits generalizability.

Descriptive Statistics

Means and standard deviations for each subscale are given for 331 males and 633 females (Franzoi & Shields, 1984), and for 54 males and 193 females (Franzoi & Herzog, 1986). No information is given about the symmetry of the distributions. Also, no information is given regarding what size of interscale difference would be significant for an individual, which would be needed if individual profiles are to be interpreted.

Reliability

Internal Consistency
Alpha coefficients for males range from .81 to .86, those for females, from .78 to .87.

Test-Retest
I found no test-retest reliability values and no indication whether mean shifts occur at retest.

Construct Validity

Irrelevant Response/Score Determiners
Forced-choice format, ipsative scoring, item overlap, item ambiguity, dichotomous scoring, and use of two-part indices (dis-

crepancy scores), with their attendant threats to validity, were avoided.

There is insufficient information to evaluate the possible influences of social-desirability and acquiescent response sets or of skewness (with the possibility that low scores may represent either unreliable responding or poor body esteem).

Convergent and Discriminant Validity

Multitrait-multimethod matrices. I found no such analyses.

Convergent validity coefficients. As evidence of convergent validity, the authors present "moderate" correlations (.19 to .51) between RSE scores and each of the three BES subscales (Franzoi & Shields, 1984; Franzoi & Herzog, 1986). However, the RSE scale is not an appropriate convergent-validity criterion for specific-aspect scales. The fact that these correlations are only moderate might better be interpreted as indicating discriminant validity of the BES scales.

No appropriate convergent validity coefficients are presented.

Discriminant validity. More explicitly relevant evidence for discriminant validity includes the following: (1) As predicted, only the Weight Concern subscale discriminated 11 anorexic females from 88 nonanorexic ones (Franzoi & Shields, 1984). (2) As predicted, only the Upper Body Strength Scale discriminated 39 male weight lifters from 41 non-weight-lifting males (Franzoi & Shields, 1984). (3) The amount of aerobic exercise for 193 females correlated only with Physical Condition scores, and for 150 males it correlated most highly with Physical Condition (but also with the other two scales [Franzoi & Herzog, 1986]). (4) As predicted, private and public body consciousness scales were only weakly correlated with BES scales (Franzoi & Herzog, 1986). (5) For women, Sexual Attractiveness scores were more strongly related to a single sexiness self-rating scale than to a single physical attractiveness (i.e., good-looking) self-rating scale. Weight Concern was strongly related to both self-ratings, but Physical Condition was less strongly related to either self-rating. Corresponding analyses for males were not clearly interpretable (Franzoi & Herzog, 1986). (6) For both genders, a four-item body competence measure correlated with all three scales, but most highly with Physical Condition (Franzoi & Herzog, 1986).

Three of the data sets above correlate two self-reports, limiting their interpretability.

11

SELF-PERCEPTION PROFILE
FOR CHILDREN (SPPC)
(Harter, 1985a)
A REVISION OF THE PERCEIVED
COMPETENCE SCALE FOR CHILDREN (PCSC)
(Harter, 1979, 1982)

Rationale and General Description

This instrument for elementary-school and preadolescent children includes a Global Self-Worth scale and five "domain-specific" scales that are factorially distinct: Scholastic Competence, Social Acceptance, Athletic Competence, Physical Appearance, and Behavioral Conduct. The latter refers to the degree to which children see themselves as doing the right thing, avoiding trouble, doing what they are supposed to do. Every scale contains six items, with each item self-evaluation to be made on a 4-step rating scale.

The SPPC is in the early stages of validation and use, but it is included here because it is the only United States self-concept scale to use factor analysis to verify a priori item selection for allegedly distinct domains and to include both domain-specific and general self-esteem scales.

The instrument is based on the following views expressed by Harter: (1) Self-conceptions about competence are especially important for such children, both in a domain-specific sense and with respect to the contributions such specific self-conceptions may make to the child's perceived global self-worth (Harter, 1985c). (2) "Recent research (Harter, 1985b) has revealed that global self-worth judgment is qualitatively different from self-descriptions in each of the 5 specific domains [of the SPPC], although it is influenced by certain domain-specific judgments"

(Harter, 1985a, p. 18). The Global Self-Worth scale "is *not* a measure of general competence" (Harter, 1985a, p. 6). (3) "It had been our conviction, derived from general developmental theory, that children would not be able to make meaningful judgments about their self-worth as a person until approximately the age of 8. The very concept of personness is not yet firmly established among younger children" (Harter, 1985b, pp. 144–145).

Item/Scale Selection and Refinement

The particular competence areas to be included were determined by "our own observations of the mastery behaviors most salient for elementary school children. . . . Interviews with children were then designed to determine which activities within these domains were particularly important to children in making judgments of competence" (Harter, 1982, p. 88).

The aim was to create an instrument with scales that are factorially distinct because of their a priori substantive conceptualizations and because of the construction of plausibly valid items for each scale, as defined conceptually. This approach is similar to that taken by Marsh and his colleagues (Marsh, Smith, & Barnes, 1983) when creating the SDQ for Australian respondents; and it is distinct from Piers's (1984) use of factor analysis *after* the PH scale was built, in order to see whether PH cluster scales measuring different aspects of self-concept could be delineated in addition to the total self-esteem score obtained by summing across items from disparate content areas. (The SDQ and the PH are reviewed in this book.) The SPPC items appear in Harter (1985a), which is available from Harter at the University of Denver.

Samples

Standardization samples comprised four groups, ranging from lower-middle to upper-middle class, 90% white, jointly including children from grades 3–8, all from Colorado. (Total $N = 1,543$—789 girls and 754 boys [Harter, 1985a].) In view of the homogeneity of the sample with respect to geographical and ethnic variables, the generalizability of psychometric information based on the standardization sample remains to be determined.

Descriptive Statistics

Subscale means and standard deviations are given by grade and gender (Harter, 1985a). Out of 144 means, 143 fall above the scale midpoint of 2.5. This fact, in conjunction with the SD values, suggests that the distributions are negatively skewed.

The manual (Harter, 1985a) provides a profile form for use with an individual child, but information is not at hand as to how large an individual's interscale difference must be to warrant the interpretation that it is reliable.

Reliability

Internal Consistency
Twenty-four alpha coefficients are given (six scales x four samples). The means for the subscales are Scholastic Competence, .82; Social Acceptance, .78; Athletic Competence, .83; Physical Appearance, .80; Behavioral Conduct, .74; Global Self-Worth, .80 (Harter, 1985a).

Test-Retest
I found no test-retest reliability values.

Construct Validity

Factor-Analytic Checks on Dimensionality
Three factor analyses were performed on the domain-specific items, one using a sixth- and seventh-grade sample, one a sixth-seventh-, and eighth-grade sample, and one a fifth- and sixth-grade sample, with $Ns = 748$, 390, and 110, respectively. In all three analyses, five factors were obtained, items loaded highly on the predicted target factor (range .33 to .80), and there were no cross-loadings greater than .18.

Interestingly, a four-factor solution was obtained in two

samples of third and fourth graders, but the nature of the factor solution for the domain-specific items differed between samples. It is suggested that for younger children "the particular content of the factors that do emerge . . . may well vary from sample to sample, depending upon the subject population, the particular milieu, as well as the educational philosophy espoused by the school administration" (Harter, 1985a, p. 18).

Six sets of intercorrelations between subscales are given, with samples ranging from grades 3–4 to 6–8. Mean interscale rs range from .14 (Athletic Competence vs. Behavioral Conduct) to .45 (Scholastic Competence vs. Behavioral Conduct). The mean for the entire matrix is .32. This amount of correlation is to be expected among scales whose items define oblique factors.

Regarding the omission of the Global Self-Worth scores from her factor analyses, Harter (1985a) argues, "Since the particular domains of importance vary from individual to individual, and thus bear a different relationship to self-worth, it becomes unlikely that self-worth will systematically emerge as a distinctive factor" (p. 18). However, one may question the logic of this assumption. Moreover, a separate self-esteem factor was found by Marsh, Smith, and Barnes (1985) and by Marsh and Gouvernet (in press) in their factor analyses of item pairs from the seven SDQ domain-specific scales plus a modified Rosenberg Self-Esteem Scale. The correlation of this self-esteem factor with each of the seven domain-specific factors exceeded the median r in the rest of the matrix. These results tend to support the Shavelson hierarchical model, and they suggest that factor analyses including *all* of Harter's items might yield similar interfactor correlation patterns, also congruent with a multifaceted, hierarchical model of self-concept. In fact, Harter's inter*scale* rs from five samples (given below under Convergent and Discriminant Validity) do follow the pattern of the interfactor correlations from the SDQ.

Irrelevant Response/Score Determiners
The following, with their attendant threats to validity, were avoided: item ambiguity, forced-choice format, ipsative scoring, dichotomous scoring, and item overlap between scales.

Discrepancy scores. The discrepancy scores computed by subtracting self-report scores from importance ratings cannot be recommended, for reasons explained in Cronbach and Furby (1970), Stanley (1971), and Wells and Marwell (1976).

Acquiescent response set. As illustrated below, each item presents both a negative and a positive wording of the characteristic it represents, and across items the favorable self-descriptions are sometimes at the left end of the scale, sometimes at the right.

Really true	Sort of true	Some kids have a lot of friends	BUT	Other kids don't have very many friends	Sort of true	Really true
☐	☐				☐	☐

Social-desirability response set. Harter (1985a) asserts that her item format tends to control social-desirability responding as well, because in her view the format implies that "half of the kids in the world (or in one's reference group) view themselves in one way, whereas the other half view themselves in the opposite manner. That is, this type of question format legitimizes either choice" (Harter, 1985a, p. 7).

This inference is not entirely convincing, however, either a priori or in view of the self-favorability bias. (Only 1 out of 144 means was smaller than 2.58, when the midpoint of the scale is 2.5 [Harter, 1985a].)

Harter (1985a, p. 7) argues, "Our confidence in this format is bolstered by the fact that children's verbal elaborations on the reasons for their choice indicate that they are giving accurate self-perceptions rather than socially desirable responses."

(For the earlier version of this test, she gives a correlation of .09 with the Children's Social Desirability Scale.)

Unspecified reference groups. Harter notes that the item format specifies no particular reference group for the word "kids," and this should induce caution in comparing among children or with "norms." Researchers might wish to clarify for their subjects just which "other kids" they are to use as their reference group.

Low self-evaluation scores from unreliable responding. Since 143 out of 144 means exceed the scale midpoint of 2.5 (a score that would be attained by chance responding), it is possible that "low self-evaluation" scores on this test could indicate either low self-evaluation or unreliable responding due to being unmotivated, being unable to read, or other causes. No information is available to evaluate this possibly invalidating influence on low scores.

Convergent and Discriminant Validity

No multitrait-multimethod matrix analyses are available.

Apparently no correlations have been made between any SPPC subscale scores and a plausibly corresponding subscale of some other test, for example, (1) the SPPC Scholastic subscale and the Piers-Harris cluster score Intellectual and School Status; (2) the SPPC Physical Appearance and the Piers-Harris cluster score Physical Appearance and Attributes or the SDQ Physical Appearance; or (3) the SPPC Social Acceptance and the Piers-Harris Popularity or the SDQ Peer Relations. Of course, this means correlating self-report scores, which might yield something more akin to alternate-form reliabilities than to convergent validity values. Nevertheless, useful information on all these tests would be provided by such correlations.

Also, there is apparently no information about how the Global Self-Worth scores correlate with an alternate measure of this construct such as the Rosenberg-Simmons Self-Esteem Scale (reviewed in this book). However, there is some rather close overlap of item content, so such a correlation should be viewed cautiously.

In the interscale rs from five samples, the mean correlation between specific domain *scales* and the Global Self-Worth *scale* is .52, ranging from .41 between Athletic Competence and Global Self-Worth to .67 for Physical Appearance and Global Self-Worth. These are higher than the rs among specific domains (mean $r = .34$; range $= .14$ to .45), as would be expected if the domains are factorially distinct while each contributes something important to Global Self-Worth.

There is a tendency for larger interscale rs to occur among younger children, perhaps implying that the scales have poorer discriminant validity for that age group. On the other hand, this tendency is congruent with Shavelson's model, which predicts increasing distinctiveness of self-concept facets with age.

The manual (Harter, 1985a) includes a form for teachers' ratings of children's actual behaviors (not their self-concepts) in each of the various domains, using three items per domain, which Harter (1985a) says she has found yields adequate reliability. However, no correlations between these ratings and children's domain-specific scores have been reported.

One would expect them to correlate, especially when both are referring to the same behavior domains, but such correlations would not constitute convergent and discriminant validity coefficients per se unless the teachers were aiming to infer the pupils' self-concepts. Rather, they would give information classifiable under Assumed Validity Studies.

Assumed Validity Studies

Harter (1987) reports correlations ranging from .50 to .65 between Global Self-Worth scores and perceived parental and peer regard, and rs ranging from .70 to .80 between Global Self-Worth scores and "affect" as measured by a Dimensions of Depression Scale for Children. (Details about sample size and measures are not given.)

The positivity of both sets of findings is consonant with theoretical predictions, but the large size of the affect correlations raises questions about the discriminant validity of the Global Self-Worth score.

It is desirable to have independent measures of others' regard and of child's own affect to compare with the findings above, which are based on two child self-reports of others' regard and affect. (For the earlier edition of this test, Harter [1985b] reports that 44 children nominated by teachers as showing affective and motivational symptoms of depression showed self-worth scores that were unusually low compared with the norm, and also at least one unusually low domain-specific score.)

Some of Harter's (1985b) findings that might be considered examples of assumed validity studies cannot be so evaluated because they use some discrepancy scores, for example, between self-rating on a domain and self-reported importance of that domain. As mentioned earlier, discrepancy scores cannot be psychometrically defended. See Cronbach and Furby (1970); Wells and Marwell (1976); and Wylie (1974).

12

CONCLUSIONS

When we compare the general status of self-concept measure-ment in 1974 and in 1987, we see both discouraging and encour-aging signs. As was unfortunately true in 1974, most recent research publications address substantive questions rather than methodological ones, and they seem to involve a variety of more-or-less idiosyncratic measuring instruments that have unspec-ified or inadequate psychometric characteristics. The potential contribution of good psychometric work all too often has gone unrecognized, perhaps thereby discouraging research on instru-ment development per se.

On the other hand, there is a somewhat greater recognition today of the need for appropriate instrument development, and there is a more widespread attempt to increase and evaluate the validity of self-concept indices by more sophisticated applica-tions of item analyses, factor analyses, multitrait-multimethod matrices, and various techniques for evaluating and minimizing the many possibly irrelevant response/score determiners that can decrease construct validity.

The ideal self is still important in self-concept theorizing, but the use of uninterpretable discrepancy scores (e.g., self-minus-ideal) has fortunately all but disappeared in the tests reviewed here.

Although some form of self-report appears to be the most appropriate (perhaps the only) way to try to index self-concep-tions, it seems that the most highly developed tests discussed here use very similar self-report methods, precluding a clear evaluation of the contribution of method variance to score variance. It is unfortunate that comparative psychometric data are not available from the more open-ended approaches that give subjects an opportunity to choose a personally relevant way of selecting and organizing their self-reports.

A striking feature of all the tests is the tendency for the majority of subjects to attain scores on the self-favorable end of the scale. Thus, scores that are numerically "low" in comparison with those of most respondents are actually near the middle of the range of possible scores. This means that they could have occurred from chance responding due to reading difficulties, indifference, inattention, guessing, and so on. The tests reviewed here provide no way to distinguish whether these "low" scores reflect low self-evaluation or random responding. This is crucial when it comes to using a self-concept instrument to evaluate differences between groups such as poor and good students, disadvantaged and privileged cultural groups, depressed and nondepressed persons, and so forth, since it is from the poor students, the disadvantaged groups, and the depressed persons that one would expect low scores both on the basis of low self-esteem and on the basis of random responding.

There has been some redress of the earlier tendency to focus on global self-regard (i.e., overall self-esteem, self-acceptance, self-ideal congruence) much more than on discriminable specific aspects or dimensions of self-concept.

In this connection, there has been an increase in useful discussions about the theoretical meaning of global self-esteem and its relationship to self-evaluations of more specific aspects of self-concept.

It is generally assumed that each individual's overall or global self-regard is determined by a combination of self-conceptions and self-evaluations concerning separate aspects of self in conjunction with the personal importance the individual assigns to each of these aspects.

Those who seek to measure global self-regard directly (e.g., Rosenberg, 1979) argue that their very general questions allow each person to take into account in his or her own way the relative contributions of specific self-evaluations to overall self-esteem.

A number of researchers are considering a multifaceted, hierarchical model of self-concept (Shavelson, Hubner, & Stanton, 1976). This model suggests the value of attempting to test more directly some assumptions about the relationship between global self-esteem measures and more specific self-evaluations.

Related to these issues are theoretical assumptions such as Harter's (1985a) that acquisition of more specific self-evaluations must developmentally precede the acquisition of a global concept and evaluation of oneself as a person.

It is obvious that several of the tests reviewed seem to be directed toward the same or similar dimensions of self-concept. Accordingly, giving a number of the tests to the same subject samples could provide needed information about convergent and discriminant validity of each of these apparently similar dimensional scores.

Moreover, although the reviewed tests of specific dimensions of self-concept now commendably cover more areas than did previous self-concept measures, it seems worthwhile to explore the possibility of measuring an even greater variety of specific self-concept dimensions.

It is encouraging that there is much more essential and sophisticated information about the instruments reviewed in detail than there was for those reviewed in Wylie (1974). On the other hand, none of those discussed here has been empirically evaluated in all the desirable ways. This should both induce caution among potential users of these instruments and inspire researchers to plan further explorations of the meaning and appropriate applicability of the scores obtained from them. None of the published information warrants using any of the these instruments as tools for diagnosing individuals.

References

Bachman, J. G. (1970). *Youth in transition: Vol. 2. The impact of family background and intelligence on tenth-grade boys.* Ann Arbor, MI: Survey Research Center, Institute for Social Research.

Bachman, J. G., & O'Malley, P. M. (1977). Self-esteem in young men: A longitudinal analysis of the impact of educational and occupational attainment. *Journal of Personality and Social Psychology, 35,* 365–380.

Balogun, J. A. (1986). Reliability and construct validity of the Body Cathexis Scale. *Perceptual and Motor Skills, 62,* 927–935.

Bentler, P. (1972). The Piers-Harris Self Concept Scale (The Way I Feel About Myself). In O. K. Buros (Ed.), *The seventh mental measurements yearbook* (pp. 124–126). Highland Park, NJ: Gryphon Press.

Bierer, B. (1981). *Preference for challenge among children who over-rate, under-rate, and accurately rate their cognitive competence.* Unpublished doctoral dissertation, University of Denver.

Black, W. F. (1974). Self concept as related to achievement and age in L.D. children. *Child Development, 4,* 1137–1140.

Block, J. (1965). *Challenge of response sets: Unconfounding meaning, acquiescence, and social desirability in the MMPI.* New York: Appleton-Century-Crofts.

Bolea, A. S., Felker, D. W., & Barnes, M. (1971). A pictorial self-concept scale for children in K–4. *Journal of Educational Measurement, 8,* 223–224.

Briggs, S. R., & Cheek, J. M. (1986). The role of factor analysis in the development and evaluation of personality scales. *Journal of Personality, 54,* 106–143.

Bromley, D. B. (1977). Natural language and the development of self.

In H. E. Howe, Jr. (Ed.), *Nebraska symposium on motivation* (vol. 25, pp. 117–217). Lincoln: University of Nebraska Press.

Brookover, W. B. (1962). *Self-Concept of Ability Scale.* East Lansing, MI: Educational Publication Service.

Brunn, A. C. (1975). *A study of relationships among self-concept, body-cathexis, and sociometric status of institutionalized adolescents.* Doctoral dissertation, Baylor University.

Buros, O. K. (Ed.). (1970). *Personality tests and reviews.* Highland Park, NJ: Gryphon Press.

Buros, O. K. (Ed.). (1972). *Seventh mental measurements yearbook.* Highland Park, NJ: Gryphon Press.

Buros, O. K. (Ed.). (1978). *Eighth mental measurements yearbook.* Highland Park, NJ: Gryphon Press.

Byrne, B. M. (1983). Investigating measures of self-concept. *Measurement and Evaluation in Guidance, 16,* 115–126.

Byrne, B. M. (in press a). Measuring adolescent self-concept: Factorial validity and equivalency of the SDQ III across gender. *Multivariate Behavioral Research.*

Byrne, B. M. (in press b). The Self Description Questionnaire III: Testing for equivalent factorial validity across ability. *Educational and Psychological Measurement.*

Byrne, B. M., & Schneider, B. H. (1988). Perceived Competence Scale for Children: Testing for factorial validity and invariance across age and ability. *Applied Measurement in Education, 1,* 171–187.

Byrne, B. M., & Shavelson, R. J. (1986). On the structure of adolescent self-concept. *Journal of Educational Psychology, 78,* 474–481.

Byrne, B. M., & Shavelson, R. J. (1987). Adolescent self-concept: Testing the assumption of equivalent structure across gender. *American Educational Research Journal, 24,* 365–385.

Campbell, D. T., & Fiske, D. W. (1959). Convergent and discriminant validation by the multitrait-multimethod matrix. *Psychological Bulletin, 56,* 81–105.

Carmines, E. G., & Zeller, R. A. (1979). *Reliability and validity assessment.* Beverly Hills, CA: Sage Publications.

Chapman, T. (1973). Unpublished data from five English primary schools.

Cooley, C. H. (1902). *Human nature and the social order.* New York: Scribners.

Coopersmith, S. (1981). *Coopersmith Self-Esteem Inventories.* Palo Alto, CA: Consulting Psychologists Press.

Cowan, R., Altmann, H., & Pysh, F. (1978). A validity study of selected self-concept instruments. *Measurement and Evaluation in Guidance, 10,* 211–221.

Cox, S. H. (1966). *Family background effects on personality development and social acceptance.* Unpublished doctoral dissertation, Texas Christian University.

Crandall, V. C., Katkovsky, W., & Crandall, V. J. (1965). Children's beliefs in their own control of reinforcements in intellectual-academic achievement situations. *Child Development, 36,* 91–109.

Crase, J. J., Foss, C. J., & Colbert, K. K. (1981). Children's self-concept and perception of parents' behavior. *Journal of Psychology, 108,* 297–303.

Cronbach, L. J., & Furby, L. (1970). How should we measure "change"—or should we? *Psychological Bulletin, 74,* 68–80.

Cronbach, L. J., & Meehl, P. E. (1955). Construct validity in psychological tests. *Psychological Bulletin, 52,* 281–302.

Dancer, L. S. (1985). On the multi-dimensional structure of self-esteem: Facet analysis of Rosenberg's Self-Esteem Scale. In D. B. Canter (Ed.), *Facet theory: Approaches to social research.* New York: Springer-Verlag.

Davis, E. E., Dokecki, P. R., Coleman, J. M., Smith, M. D., & Wood, L. (1975, January). *The PASS Model Project: Development, evaluation, and dissemination of a service delivery system for learning disabilities.* Paper presented at the meeting of the International Federation on Learning Disabilities, Brussels.

Demo, D. H. (1985). The measurement of self-esteem: Refining our methods. *Journal of Personality and Social Psychology, 48,* 1490–1502.

Devoe, M. W. (1977). Cooperation as a function of self-concept, sex, and race. *Educational Research Quarterly, 2,* 3–8.

Dickstein, E. (1977). Self and self-esteem: Theoretical foundations and their implications for research. *Human Development, 20,* 129–140.

Dobson, C., Goudy, W. J., Keith, P. M., & Powers, E. (1979). Further analysis of Rosenberg's Self-Esteem Scale. *Psychological Reports, 44,* 639–641.

Eastman, E. (1965). *The relationship between self-concept and intelligence in children.* Unpublished research paper, Whitworth College, Spokane, WA.

Elkind, D., & Bowen, R. (1979). Imaginary audience behavior in children and adolescents. *Developmental Psychology, 15,* 38–44.

Epstein, J. (1985). Review of Piers-Harris Self-Concept Scale. In J. V.

Mitchell (Ed.), *Ninth mental measurements yearbook* (pp. 1168–1169). Lincoln: University of Nebraska Press.

Farls, R. (1966). Unpublished data received from Freedom Area School District, Freedom, PA

Felker, D. W., & Thomas, S. B. (1971). Self-initiated verbal reinforcement and positive self-concept. *Child Development, 42,* 1285–1287.

Fiske, D. W. (1966). Some hypotheses concerning test adequacy. *Educational and Psychological Measurement, 26,* 69–88.

Fitts, W. H. (1965). *Tennessee Self-Concept Scale: Manual.* Los Angeles, CA: Western Psychological Services.

Fleming, J. S., & Courtney, B. E. (1984). The dimensionality of self-esteem: II. Hierarchical facet model for revised measurement scales. *Journal of Personality and Social Psychology, 46,* 404–421.

Franklin, M. R., Duley, S. M., Rousseau, E. W., & Sabers, D. L. (1981). Construct validation of the Piers-Harris Children's Self-Concept Scale. *Educational and Psychological Measurement, 41,* 439–443.

Franzoi, S. L., & Herzog, M. E. (1986). The Body Esteem Scale: A convergent and discriminant validity study. *Journal of Personality Assessment, 50,* 24–31.

Franzoi, S. L., & Herzog, M. E. (1987). Judging physical attractiveness: What body aspects do we use? *Personality and Social Psychology Bulletin, 13,* 19–33.

Franzoi, S. L., & Shields, S. A. (1984). The Body Esteem Scale: Multidimensional structure and sex differences in a college population. *Journal of Personality Assessment, 48,* 173–178.

Goldsmith, R. E. (1985). The factorial composition of the Kirton Adaption-Innovation Inventory. *Educational and Psychological Measurement, 45,* 245–250.

Goodenough, F. (1938). The use of pronouns by young children: A note on the development of self-awareness. *Journal of Genetic Psychology, 52,* 333–346.

Gould, J. (1982). A psychometric investigation of the standard and short form Beck Depression Inventory. *Psychological Reports, 51,* 1167–1170.

Guiton, G., & Zachary, R. A. (1984, August). *Criterion validity of the Piers-Harris Children's Self-Concept Scale.* Paper presented at the annual meeting of the American Psychological Association, Toronto.

Gullo, D. F., & Ambrose, R. P. (1987). Perceived competence and social acceptance in kindergarten: Its relation to academic performance. *Journal of Educational Research, 81*, 28–32.

Guterman, S. S. (1982). Are personality tests equally valid within different social classes? A case study using locus of control. *International Journal of Contemporary Sociology, 19*, 139–173.

Guyot, G. W., Fairchild, L., & Johnson, B. (1984). Embedded Figures Test performance and self-concept of elementary school children. *Perceptual and Motor Skills, 58*, 61–62.

Hammond, S., & O'Rourke, M. M. (1984). A psychometric investigation into the Body-Cathexis Scale. *Personality and Individual Differences, 5*, 603–605.

Harder, D. W., Strauss, J. S., Kokes, R. F., & Ritzler, B. A. (1984). Self-derogation and psychopathology. *Genetic Psychology Monographs, 109*, 223–249.

Harman, H. H. (1967). *Modern factor analysis* (2nd ed.). Chicago: University of Chicago Press.

Harter, S. (1978). Effectance motivation reconsidered: Toward a developmental model. *Human Development, 1*, 34–64.

Harter, S. (1979). *Manual: Perceived Competence Scale for Children*. Denver, CO: University of Denver.

Harter, S. (1982). The Perceived Competence Scale for Children. *Child Development, 53*, 87–97.

Harter, S. (1985a). *Manual for the Self-Perception Profile for Children (revision of the Perceived Competence Scale for Children)*. Denver, CO: University of Denver.

Harter, S. (1985b). Processes underlying the construction, maintenance, and enhancement of self-concept in children. In J. Suls & A. Greenwald (Eds.), *Psychological perspectives on the self* (vol. 3, pp. 137–181). Hillsdale, NJ: Lawrence Erlbaum.

Harter, S. (1985c). Competence as a dimension of self-evaluation. In R. L. Leahy (Ed.), *The development of self* (pp. 48–122). Orlando, FL: Academic Press.

Harter, S. (1987). The determinants and mediational role of global self-worth in children. In N. Eisenberg (Ed.), *Contemporary topics in developmental psychology* (pp. 219–242). New York: Wiley.

Harter, S., & Pike, R. (1981). *The Pictorial Scale of Perceived Competence and Acceptance for Young Children: Plates for First and Second Grades*. Denver, CO: University of Denver.

Harter, S., & Pike, R. (1983). *The Pictorial Scale of Perceived Competence and Social Acceptance for Young Children: Procedural Manual*. Denver, CO: University of Denver.

Harter, S., & Pike, R. (1984). The pictorial perceived competence scale for young children. *Child Development, 55,* 1969–1982.

Hensley, W. E. (1977). Differences between males and females on the Rosenberg Scale of Self-Esteem. *Psychological Reports, 41,* 829–830.

Hensley, W. E., & Roberts, M. K. (1976). Dimensions of Rosenberg's Scale of Self-Esteem. *Psychological Reports, 38,* 583–584.

Hoffman, D. A. (1976). Cognitive style and intelligence: Their relationship to leadership and self-concept (doctoral dissertation, Ohio State University, 1975). *Dissertation Abstracts International, 36,* 4133 B (University Microfilms No. 76–3454, 118).

Hojat, M. (1982). Loneliness as a function of selected personality variables. *Journal of Clinical Psychology, 38,* 137–141.

Hughes, C. S. (1971). *Self-esteem and achievement as related to elementary school reporting instruments.* Unpublished doctoral dissertation, Kent State University.

Humphreys, L. G. (1960). Note on the multitrait-multimethod matrix. *Psychological Bulletin, 57,* 86–88.

Jackson, D. N. (1969). Multimethod factor analysis in the evaluation of convergent and discriminant validity. *Psychological Bulletin, 72,* 30–49.

Jackson, S. A., & Marsh, H. W. (1986). Athletic or antisocial? The female sport experience. *Journal of Sport Psychology, 8,* 198–211.

Jersild, A. T. (1952). *In search of self.* New York: Teachers College Bureau of Publications.

Jeske, P. J. (1985). Review of Piers-Harris Self-Concept Scale. In J. V. Mitchell (Ed.), *Ninth mental measurements yearbook* (pp. 1169–1170). Lincoln: University of Nebraska Press.

Johnson, B. W., Redfield, D. L., Miller, R. L., & Simpson, R. E. (1983). The Coopersmith Self-Esteem Inventory: A construct validation study. *Educational and Psychological Measurement, 43,* 907–913.

Joseph, J. (1979). *Pre-school and Primary Self-Concept Screening Test: Instruction Manual.* Chicago: Stoelting.

Judd, C. M., Jessor, R., & Donovan, J. E. (1986). Structural equation models and personality research. *Journal of Personality, 54,* 149–198.

Kanoy, R. C., Johnson, B. W., & Kanoy, K. W. (1980). Locus of control and self-concept in achieving and underachieving bright elementary students. *Psychology in the Schools, 17,* 395–399.

Kaplan, H. B. (1978). Social class, self-derogation and deviant response. *Social Psychiatry, 13,* 19–28.

Kaplan, H. B., & Pokorny, A. D. (1969). Self-derogation and psychosocial adjustment. *Journal of Nervous and Mental Disease, 149,* 421–434.

Karnes, F. A., & Wherry, J. N. (1982). Concurrent validity of the Children's Personality Questionnaire O Factor as suggested by the Piers-Harris Children's Self-Concept Scale. *Psychological Reports, 50,* 574.

Kavanagh, M. J., MacKinney, A. C., & Wolins, L. (1971). Issues in managerial performance: Multitrait-multimethod analyses of ratings. *Psychological Bulletin, 75,* 34–49.

Keller, R. T., & Holland, W. E. (1978). A cross-validation study of the Kirton Adaption Inventory in three research and development organizations. *Applied Psychological Measurement, 2,* 563–570.

Ketcham, B., & Snyder, R. T. (1977). Self-attitudes of the intellectually and socially advantaged student: Normative study of the Piers-Harris Children's Self-Concept Scale. *Psychological Reports, 40,* 111–116.

Kihlstrom, J. F., & Cantor, N. (1984). Mental representations of the self. In L. Berkowitz (Ed.), *Advances in experimental social psychology* (vol. 17, pp. 1–47). New York: Academic Press.

Kinnier, R. T. (1987). Development of a Values Conflict Resolution Assessment. *Journal of Counseling Psychology, 34,* 31–37.

Kohn, M. L. (1969). *Class and conformity: A study in values.* Homewood, IL: Dorsey Press.

L'Écuyer, R. (1975). *La genèse du concept de soi: Théorie et recherches.* Sherbrooke, Quebec: Editions Naaman de Sherbrooke.

L'Écuyer, R. (1981). The development of the self-concept through the life span. In M. D. Lynch, A. A. Norem-Hebeisen, & K. Gergen (Eds.), *Self-concept: Advances in theory and research* (pp. 203–218). Cambridge, MA: Bollinger.

Livesely, M. J., & Bromley, D. B. (1973). *Person perception in childhood and adolescence.* London: Wiley.

Lord, S. B. (1971). *Self-concepts of Appalachian children: A comparative study of economically poor and economically advantaged children using the Piers-Harris Self-Concept Inventory.* Doctoral dissertation, Indiana University.

Lorr, M., & Wunderlich, R. A. (1986). Two objective measures of self-esteem. *Journal of Personality Assessment, 50,* 18–23.

Mannarino, A. P. (1978). Friendship patterns and self-concept development in preadolescent males. *Journal of Genetic Psychology, 133,* 105–110.

Markus, H., & Nurius, P. (1986). Possible selves. *American Psychologist, 41*, 954–969.

Markus, H., & Nurius, P. (1987). Possible selves: The interface between motivation and the self-concept. In K. Yardley & T. Honess (Eds.), *Self and identity: Psychosocial perspectives* (pp. 157–172). London: Routledge & Kegan Paul.

Marsh, H. W. (1984a). Relations among dimensions of self-attribution, dimensions of self-concept and academic achievements. *Journal of Educational Psychology, 76*, 1291–1308.

Marsh, H. W. (1984b). Self-concept: The application of a frame-of-reference model to explain paradoxical results. *Australian Journal of Education, 28*, 165–181.

Marsh, H. W. (1985). Age and sex effects in multiple dimensions of preadolescent self-concept: A replication and extension. *Australian Journal of Psychology, 37*, 197–204.

Marsh, H. W. (1986a). Global self-esteem: Its relation to specific facets of self-concept and their importance. *Journal of Personality and Social Psychology, 51*, 1224–1236.

Marsh, H. W. (1986b). Verbal and math self-concepts: An internal/external frame of reference model. *American Educational Research Journal, 23*, 129–149.

Marsh, H. W. (1986c). Negative item bias in ratings scales for preadolescent children: A cognitive-developmental phenomenon. *Developmental Psychology, 22*, 37–49.

Marsh, H. W. (1986d). The self-serving effect (bias?) in academic attributions: Its relation to academic achievement and self-concept. *Journal of Educational Psychology, 78*, 190–200.

Marsh, H. W. (1987a). Masculinity, femininity, and androgyny: Their relations with multiple dimensions of self-concept. *Multivariate Behavioral Research, 22*, 91–118.

Marsh, H. W. (1987b). The factorial invariance of responses by males and females to a multidimensional self-concept instrument: Substantive and methodolological issues. *Multivariate Behavioral Research, 22*, 457–480.

Marsh, H. W. (1987c). The hierarchical structure of self-concept: An application of hierarchical confirmatory analysis. *Journal of Educational Measurement, 24*, 17–39.

Marsh, H. W. (in press a). *The Self-Description Questionnaire SDQ: A theoretical and empirical basis for the measurement of multiple dimensions of preadolescent self-concept: A test manual and a research monograph.* San Antonio, TX: Psychological Corporation.

Marsh, H. W. (in press b). *The Self Description Questionnaire (SDQ) II: A theoretical and empirical basis for the measurement of multiple dimensions of adolescent self-concept: An interim test manual and a research monograph.* San Antonio, TX: Psychological Corporation.

Marsh, H. W. (in press c). *The Self Description Questionnaire (SDQ) III: A theoretical and empirical basis for the measurement of multiple dimensions of late adolescent self-concept: An interim test manual and a research monograph.* San Antonio, TX: Psychological Corporation.

Marsh, H. W. (in review). Age and sex effects in multiple dimensions of self-concept: Preadolescence to early adulthood.

Marsh, H. W., Barnes, J., Cairns, L., & Tidman, M. (1984). Self-Description Questionnaire: Age and sex effects in the structure and level of self-concept for preadolescent children. *Journal of Educational Psychology, 76*, 940–956.

Marsh, H. W., Barnes, J., & Hocevar, D. (1985). Self-other agreement on multidimensional self-concept ratings: Factor analysis and multitrait-multimethod analysis. *Journal of Personality and Social Psychology, 49*, 1360–1377.

Marsh, H. W., Byrne, B. M., & Shavelson, R. J. (in press). A multifaceted academic self-concept: Its hierarchical structure and its relation to academic achievement. *Journal of Educational Psychology.*

Marsh, H. W., Cairns, L., Relich, J., Barnes, J., & Debus, R. L. (1984). The relationship between dimensions of self-attribution and dimensions of self-concept. *Journal of Educational Psychology, 76*, 3–32.

Marsh, H. W., & Gouvernet, P. (in press). Multidimensional self-concepts and perceptions of control: Construct validation of responses by children. *Journal of Educational Psychology.*

Marsh, H. W., & Hocevar, D. (1983). Confirmatory factor analysis of multitrait-multimethod matrices. *Journal of Educational Measurement, 20*, 231–248.

Marsh, H. W., & Hocevar, D. (1985). Application of confirmatory factor analysis to the study of self-concept: First and higher-order models and their invariance across groups. *Psychological Bulletin, 97*, 562–582.

Marsh, H. W., & Jackson, S. (1986). Multidimensional self-concepts, masculinity and femininity as a function of women's involvement in athletics. *Sex Roles, 15*, 391–416.

Marsh, H. W., & O'Neill, R. (1984). Self-Description Questionnaire III (SDQ III): The construct validity of multidimensional self-concept ratings by late adolescents. *Journal of Educational Measurement, 24,* 153–174.

Marsh, H. W., & Parker, J. (1984). Determinants of student self-concept: Is it better to be a relatively large fish in a small pond even if you don't learn to swim as well? *Journal of Personality and Social Psychology, 47,* 213–231.

Marsh, H. W., Parker, J., & Barnes, J. (1985). Multidimensional adolescent self-concepts: Their relationship to age, sex, and academic measures. *American Educational Research Journal, 22,* 422–444.

Marsh, H. W., Parker, J. W., & Smith, I. D. (1983). Preadolescent self-concept: Its relation to self-concept as inferred by teachers and to academic ability. *British Journal of Educational Psychology, 53,* 60–78.

Marsh, H. W., & Peart, N. (in press). Competitive and cooperative physical fitness training programs for girls: Effects on physical fitness and on multidimensional self-concepts. *Journal of Sport Psychology.*

Marsh, H. W., Relich, J. D., & Smith, I. D. (1983). Self-concept: The construct validity of interpretations based upon the SDQ. *Journal of Personality and Social Psychology, 45,* 173–187.

Marsh, H. W., & Richards, G. E. (in press a). The Tennessee Self Concept Scale: Reliability, internal structure, and construct validity. *Journal of Personality and Social Psychology.*

Marsh, H. W., & Richards, G. E. (in press b). The Outward Bound Bridging Course for low achieving high-school males: Effect on academic achievement and multidimensional self-concepts. *Australian Journal of Psychology.*

Marsh, H. W., Richards, G. E., & Barnes, J. (1986a). Multidimensional self-concepts: The effect of participation in an Outward Bound program. *Journal of Personality and Social Psychology, 50,* 195–204.

Marsh, H. W., Richards, G. E., & Barnes, J. (1986b). Multidimensional self-concepts: A long-term follow-up of the effect of participation in the Outward Bound program. *Personality and Social Psychology Bulletin, 12,* 475–492.

Marsh, H. W., & Shavelson, R. J. (1985). Self-concept: Its multifaceted, hierarchical structure. *Educational Psychologist, 20,* 107–125.

Marsh, H. W., & Smith, I. D. (1987). A cross-national study of the structure and level of multidimensional self-concepts: An application of confirmatory analysis. *Australian Journal of Psychology, 39,* 61–77.

Marsh, H. W., Smith, I. D., & Barnes, J. (1983). Multitrait-multi-method analyses of the Self-Description Questionnaire: Student-teacher agreement on multidimensional ratings of student self-concept. *American Educational Research Journal, 20,* 333–357.

Marsh, H. W., Smith, I. D., & Barnes, J. (1984). Multidimensional self-concepts: Relationships with inferred self-concepts and academic achievement. *Australian Journal of Psychology, 36,* 367–386.

Marsh, H. W., Smith, I. D., & Barnes, J. (1985). Multidimensional self-concepts: Relations with sex and academic achievement. *Journal of Educational Psychology, 77,* 581–596.

Marsh, H. W., Smith, I. D., Barnes, J., & Butler, S. (1983). Self-concept: Reliability, dimensionality, and validity, and the measurement of change. *Journal of Educational Psychology, 75,* 772–790.

Marsh, H. W., Smith, I. D., Myers, M. R., & Owens, L. (in press). The transition from single-sex to coeducational high schools: Effects on multiple dimensions of self-concept and on academic achievement. *American Educational Research Journal.*

Mayer, C. L. (1965). *A study of the relationship of early special class placement and the self-concepts of mentally handicapped children.* Unpublished doctoral dissertation, Syracuse University.

McGuire, W. J., & McGuire, C. V. (1987). Developmental trends and gender differences in the subjective experience of self. In T. Honess & K. Yardley (Eds.), *Self and identity: Perspective across the life span* (pp. 134–146). London: Routledge & Kegan Paul.

McIntire, W. G., & Drummond, R. J. (1977). Multiple predictors of self-concept in children. *Psychology in the Schools, 14,* 295–298.

McIver, J. P., & Carmines, E. G. (1981). *Unidimensional scaling.* Sage University Paper Series on Quantitative Application in the Social Sciences, Series No. 07–024. Beverly Hills, CA: Sage Publications.

Mettes, D. (1974). *Self-report vs. teacher observation.* Unpublished manuscript, Purdue University, Lafayette, IN.

Michael, W. B., Smith, R. A., & Michael, J. J. (1975). The factorial validity of the Piers-Harris Children's Self-Concept Scale for each of three samples of elementary, junior high, and senior high school students in a large metropolitan school district. *Educational and Psychological Measurement, 35,* 404–414.

Millen, L. (1966). *The relationship between self-concept, social desirability, and anxiety in children.* Unpublished master's thesis, Pennsylvania State University.

Mitchell, J. V. (Ed.). (1985). *Ninth mental measurements yearbook*. Lincoln: University of Nebraska Press.

Moyal, B. R. (1977). Locus of control, self-esteem, stimulus appraisal, and depressive symptoms in children. *Journal of Consulting and Clinical Psychology, 45*, 951–952.

O'Brien, E. J. (1985). Global self-esteem: Unidimensional or multidimensional? *Psychological Reports, 57*, 383–389.

Orme, J. G., Reis, J., & Herz, E. J. (1986). Factorial and discriminant validity of the Center for Epidemiological Studies Depression (CES-D) Scale. *Journal of Clinical Psychology, 42*, 28–33.

Osborne, W. L., & LeGette, H. R. (1982). Sex, race, grade level, and social class difference in self-concept. *Measurement and Evaluation in Guidance, 14*, 195–201.

Parish, T. S., & Taylor, J. C. (1978a). The Personal Attribute Inventory for Children: A report on its validity and reliability as a self-concept scale. *Educational and Psychological Measurement, 38*, 565–569.

Parish, T. S., & Taylor, J. C. (1978b). A further report on the validity and reliability of the Personal Attributes Inventory for Children as a self-concept scale. *Educational and Psychological Measurement, 38*, 1225–1228.

Piers, E. V. (1963). Unpublished factor analysis data for the Piers-Harris Children's Self-Concept Scale.

Piers, E. V. (1965). *Children's self-rating and rating by others*. Unpublished manuscript.

Piers, E. V. (1973). Unpublished data for the Piers-Harris Children's Self-Concept Scale.

Piers. E. V. (1977). Children's self-esteem, level of esteem certainty, and responsibility for success and failure. *Journal of Genetic Psychology, 130*, 295–304.

Piers, E. V. (1984). *Piers-Harris Children's Self-Concept Scale: Revised Manual*. Los Angeles, CA: Western Psychological Services.

Piers, E. V., & Harris, D. B. (1964). Age and other correlates of self-concept in children. *Journal of Educational Psychology, 55*, 91–95.

Pihl, R. O., Parkes, M., Drake, H., & Vrana, F. (1980). The intervention of a modulator with learning disabled children. *Journal of Clinical Psychology, 36*, 972–976.

Platten, M. R., & Williams, L. R. (1979). A comparative analysis of the factorial structures of two administrations of the Piers-Harris Self-Concept Scale to one group of elementary school children. *Educational and Psychological Measurement, 39*, 471–478.

Platten, M. R., & Williams, L. R. (1981). Replication of a test-retest factorial validity study with the Piers-Harris Children's Self-Concept Scale. *Educational and Psychological Measurement, 41,* 453–462.

Querry, P. H. (1970). *A study of the self-concept of children with functional articulation disorders and normal children.* Unpublished master's thesis, University of Pittsburgh.

Reck, U. M. (1980). Self-concept, school, and social setting: A comparison of rural Appalachian and urban non-Appalachian sixth graders. *Journal of Educational Research, 74,* 49–54.

Rich, C. E., Barcikowski, R. S., & Witmer, J. M. (1979). The factorial validity of the Piers-Harris Children's Self-Concept Scale for a sample of intermediate-level EMR students enrolled in elementary school. *Educational and Psychological Measurement, 39,* 485–490.

Rosenberg, M. (1965). *Society and the adolescent self-image.* Princeton, NJ: Princeton University Press.

Rosenberg, M. (1979). *Conceiving the self.* New York: Basic Books.

Rosenberg, M., & Simmons, R. G. (1972). *Black and white self-esteem: The urban school child.* Washington, DC: American Sociological Association.

Rotundo, N., & Hensley, V. R. (1985). The Children's Depression Scale: A study of its validity. *Journal of Child Psychology and Psychiatry and Allied Disciplines, 26,* 917–927.

Saylor, C. F., Finch, A. J., Jr., Baskin, C. H., Furey, W., & Kelly, M. M. (1984). Construct validity for measures of childhood depression: Application of multitrait-multimethod methodology. *Journal of Consulting and Clinical Psychology, 52,* 977–985.

Schauer, G. H. (1975). *An analysis of the self-report of fifth and sixth grade regular class children and gifted class children.* Unpublished doctoral dissertation, Kent State University.

Schmitt, N., & Bedeian, A. G. (1982). A comparison of LISREL and two-stage least squares analysis of a hypothesized life-job satisfaction reciprocal relationship. *Journal of Applied Psychology, 67,* 806–817.

Secord, P. F., & Jourard, S. M. (1953). The appraisal of body-cathexis: Body-cathexis and the self. *Journal of Psychology, 17,* 343–347.

Shavelson, R. J., & Bolus, R. (1982). Self-concept: The interplay of theory and methods. *Journal of Educational Psychology, 74,* 3–17.

Shavelson, R. J., Hubner, J. J., & Stanton, G. C. (1976). Self-concept: Validation of construct interpretations. *Review of Educational Research, 46,* 407–441.

Sheare, J. B. (1978). The impact of resource programs upon the self-concept and peer acceptance of learning disabled children. *Psychology in the Schools, 15*, 406–412.

Shorkey, C. T., & Whiteman, V. L. (1978). Correlations between standard English and dialectical Spanish versions of five personality scales. *Psychological Reports, 43*, 910.

Silber, E., & Tippett, J. (1965). Self-esteem: Clinical assessment and measurement validation. *Psychological Reports, 16*, 1017–1071.

Simmons, R. G., & Blyth, D. A. (1987). *Moving into adolescence: The impact of pubertal change and school context.* New York: Aldine De Gruyter.

Simmons, R. G., Blyth, D. A., Van Cleave, E. F., & Bush, D. M. (1979). Entry into early adolescence: The impact of school structure, puberty, and early dating on self-esteem. *American Sociological Review, 44*, 948–967.

Simmons, R. G., Brown, L., Bush, D. M., & Blyth, D. A. (1978). Self-esteem and achievement of black and white adolescents. *Social Problems, 26*, 86–96.

Simmons, R. G., Rosenberg, F., & Rosenberg, M. (1973). Disturbance in the self-image at adolescence. *American Sociological Review, 38*, 553–568.

Smith, M. D., & Rogers, C. M. (1977). Item instability on the Piers-Harris Children's Self-Concept Scale for academic underachievers with high, middle, and low self-concepts. *Educational and Psychological Measurement, 37*, 553–558.

Smith, M. D., Zingale, S. A., & Coleman, J. M. (1978). The influence of adult expectancy/child performance discrepancies upon children's self-concepts. *American Educational Research Journal, 15*, 259–265.

Soares, A. T., & Soares, L. M. (1979). *The Affective Perception Inventory—Advanced Level.* Trumbull, CT: ALSO.

Stanley, J. C. (1971). Reliability. In R. L. Thorndike (Ed.), *Educational measurement* (2nd ed.) (pp. 356–442). Washington, DC: American Council on Education.

Stopper, C. J. (1978). *The relationships of self-concept of gifted and nongifted elementary school students to achievement, sex, grade level, and membership in a self-contained academic program for the gifted.* Newton, PA: Marple Newton School District.

Strauss, C. C., Forehand, R. L., Frame, C., & Smith, K. (1984). Characteristics of children with extreme scores on the Children's

Depression Inventory. *Journal of Clinical Child Psychology, 13,* 227–231.

Tavormina, J. B. (1975, April). *Chronically ill children: A psychologically and emotionally deviant population.* Paper presented to the Society for Research in Child Development, Denver.

Thomas, T. A. (1984). *An investigation into the influence of anxiety and the effectiveness of treatments involving positive coping skills to alleviate anxiety's detrimental effects.* Unpublished B.A. honours thesis in education, University of Sydney, Australia.

Tucker, L. A. (1981). Internal structure, factor satisfaction, and reliability of the Body Cathexis Scale. *Perceptual and Motor Skills, 53,* 891–896.

Tucker, L. A. (1982). Relationship between perceived somatotype and body cathexis of college males. *Psychological Reports, 50,* 983–989.

Ward, R. A. (1977). The impact of subjective age and stigma on older persons. *Journal of Gerontology, 32,* 227–232.

Wells, L. E., & Marwell, G. (1976). *Self-esteem: Its conceptualization and measurement.* Beverly Hills, CA: Sage Publications.

Wheeler, V. A., & Ladd, G. W. (1982). Assessment of children's self-efficacy for social interaction with peers. *Developmental Psychology, 18,* 795–805.

Whiteman, V. L. (1979). Development of an Australian version of the Rational Behavior Inventory. *Psychological Reports, 44,* 104–106.

Whiteman, V. L., & Shorkey, C. T. (1978). Validation testing of the Rational Behavior Inventory. *Educational and Psychological Measurement, 38,* 1143–1149.

Winne, P. H., Marx, R. W., & Taylor, T. D. (1977). A multitrait-multimethod study of three self-concept inventories. *Child Development, 48,* 893–901.

Wolf, T. M., Sklov, M. C., Hunter, S. M., Webber, L. S., & Berenson, G. S. (1982). Factor analytic study of the Piers-Harris Children's Self-Concept Scale. *Journal of Personality Assessment, 46,* 511–513.

Wylie, R. C. (1968). The present status of self theory. In E. A. Borgatta & W. W. Lambert (Eds.), *Handbook of personality theory and research* (pp. 728–787). Chicago: Rand McNally.

Wylie, R. C. (1974). *The self-concept: Vol. 1. A review of methodological considerations and measuring instruments* (rev. ed.). Lincoln: University of Nebraska Press.

Wylie, R. C. (1979). *The self-concept: Vol. 2. Theory and research on selected topics* (rev. ed.). Lincoln: University of Nebraska Press.

Yonker, R. J., Blixt, S., & Dinero, T. (1974). *A methodological investigation of the development of a semantic differential to assess self-concept.* Paper presented to the National Council on Measurement in Education, Chicago.

Subject and Test Index

In the index subentries, tests reviewed in this volume are referred to by initials, thus:

BES   Body Esteem Scale
JPPSST   Joseph Pre-School and Primary Self-Concept Screening Test
PH   Piers-Harris Children's Self-Concept Test
PSCA   Pictorial Scale of Perceived Competence and Social Acceptance for Young Children (Harter)
RSE   Rosenberg Self-Esteem Scale
RSSE   Rosenberg-Simmons Self-Esteem Scale
SDQ   Self-Description Questionnaire (Marsh)
SDQ II   Self-Description Questionnaire II (Marsh)
SDQ III   Self-Description Questionnaire III (Marsh)
SPPC   Self-Perception Profile for Children (Harter)

Name Index